The TEXAS RANGERS

The TEXAS RANGERS
Images and Incidents

By JOHN L. DAVIS

The University of Texas
Institute
of Texan Cultures
at San Antonio

Library of Congress Cataloging-in-Publication Data

Davis, John L.
　The Texas Rangers : images and incidents / by John L. Davis.
　　p.　　cm.
　Rev. ed. of: The Texas Rangers, their first 150 years. 1975.
　Includes bibliographical references and index.
　ISBN 0-86701-052-5. — ISBN 0-86701-053-3 (pbk.)
　　1. Texas Rangers—History.　　I. University of Texas Institute of
Texan Cultures at San Antonio.　　II. Davis, John L. Texas Rangers,
their first 150 years　　III. Title.
F391.D26　1991
363.2'09764—dc20　　　　　　　　　　　　　91-176
　　　　　　　　　　　　　　　　　　　　　　　CIP

The Texas Rangers:
　Images and Incidents
by John L. Davis

Revised edition
Copyright © 1991
The University of Texas
　Institute of Texan Cultures at San Antonio

John R. McGiffert, Executive Director 1985-1991
Rex H. Ball, Executive Director 1991-

Production Staff: Sandra Hodsdon Carr, David Haynes,
Bill Holloway, Lynn Weiss; Alice Sackett, indexer

This publication was made possible by The University of Texas System
Chancellor's Council, O. Scott and Edwina Petty, B.J. "Red" McCombs,
the Amy Shelton McNutt Trust, and Houston Endowment, Inc.

Title page photo:　*Capt. Brooks's company off on a scout, 1892*
Front cover photo:　*Capt. Jerry Gray's Company B in the Big Bend District near Marfa, 1918*
　　　　　　　(See also page 146.)
Back cover photo:　*Ranger on highway lookout, 1946*

This book is printed on Archiva acid-free paper which will not yellow with age.
Printed in the United States of America

CONTENTS

Sgt. J.R. Hunnicutt in the Big Bend area, c. 1918

FOREWORD

Texas Rangers have been critically important to the development of this state for 170 years. When trouble arose on the frontier, they met it head-on, surmounting danger and hardship to maintain law and order. They adjusted to changing conditions over time, and today they continue to serve modern Texans with dedication, zeal, and bravery. We owe them—and we need to recognize their colorful history as an integral part of our own. That history has been recorded in many ways over the years, but still deserves attention and publication. Not all the incidents are complimentary to the Ranger services; most are.

In 1975 the Institute of Texan Cultures published *The Texas Rangers: Their First 150 Years*, containing pictures and text from a 1973 Institute traveling exhibit of the same title. Since the book sold out years ago, we and the author, Dr. John L. Davis, have wanted to "do it better." But, for many reasons, a new book has not been possible till now.

At last it is ready, with new design, new material, and a direct, personal approach to the Rangers' story. The Institute is grateful to John Davis, who, though no longer on staff, gave the time and effort to complete the task. I hope you'll agree with me that he did it well.

The Texas Rangers deserve the recognition, understanding, and respect of all Texans. We believe that this book will be helpful in the achievement of that goal.

Lt. Gen. John R. McGiffert (U.S.A., ret.)
Executive Director, Institute of Texan Cultures, 1985-1991

"BLACKIE"
C.L. BLACKWELL
PRESIDIO, TEX.
1921
CO·A· UNDER
CAPT. JERRY
GRAY

C.L. "Blackie" Blackwell, Company A, Texas Rangers, at Presidio in 1921

THE TEXAS RANGERS
Images and Incidents

INTRODUCTION

When the first English-speaking colonists moved into Mexican Texas, they brought their own ways of doing things. Their customs, beliefs, laws, and institutions had developed both in England and in two centuries of American pioneering from the Atlantic coast to the Sabine River. Among the institutions was the ranger.

Since the beginning of Anglo-American expansion westward in North America, rangers had been employed: armed, mounted men who "ranged" the frontier line of farms and homesteads primarily to protect settlers from Indians or other enemies. They were often civilian volunteers, mostly un-uniformed, sometimes unpaid, and always enrolled for brief periods. In today's jargon they were small, paramilitary units raised by colonial governments or even town councils. No one intended them as substitutes for either the police or an army; they filled a different need.

Rangers could operate beyond settlement boundaries, move with great speed through a wilderness, and settle trouble right on the spot.

When Stephen F. Austin's Texas colony was threatened by Indian attacks in 1823, he called up a ranging company for its protection. Later governments did the same. During the next fifty years, rangers were not called "Texas Rangers" but were thought of as a more or less temporary frontier necessity. The frontier remained troubled, and they were more often in the field than not. Within a century after Austin's handwritten request for ten volunteers, rangers evolved into the permanent law-enforcing service they are today.

Their functions changed with the times. In the 1836 Texas Revolution, faced by the armies of Santa Anna, the ranging companies became a part of the insurgent Texan army. They rode between retreating Texas forces and advancing Mexicans, serving as a rear guard and helping civilians clear out ahead of the enemy.

Texas Rangers preparing for a scout

After the republic was established, sporadic but serious conflict between Texas and Mexico continued. Now the Rangers faced two enemies—Indians and Mexican troops. For more than a dozen years, they operated as irregular fighting units, serving as scouts, guerrillas, and cavalry support for regular soldiers, particularly between the Nueces and the Rio Grande. They also ranged the ambiguous northwestern frontier in frequent battle with Indians.

In the Mexican War Rangers enlisted as units of the United States Army. At war's end they returned to a dual role, protecting the western frontier and acting as guards on the newly established southern border of the United States, the Rio Grande. They built

San Antonio de Béxar, sketched by W. Bissett, c. 1840

a reputation for quick striking power over a vast area, often with few riders. To the Anglo-American settler and businessman, the Ranger stood for courage, peacekeeping, and frontier resourcefulness. To his opponents, he represented the use of unhesitating violence and unrelenting pursuit.

In time the Indians were killed or driven from their last footholds in Texas, and the Rio Grande—with notable exceptions—stabilized into a peaceful international border.

The next opponent was the outlaw, whatever his race or activity. Rangers were given the role of peace officers, a state police force, though never in name. They put down cattle rustling, fence cutting, mob violence . . . any breach of the law too violent or widespread for local police officers. In later years the term "outlaw" included rough characters in oil boom towns. Strike "enforcers" and contemporary gangsters—anyone breaking the established laws of the state—came under Ranger fire, often literally. At times Rangers were praised for their immediate response to trouble and effectiveness in peacekeeping; at times they were accused – even by local lawmen – of operating outside any imaginable jurisdiction and delighting in the use of excessive force.

The number of Rangers in the field varied over the years according to need, legal restrictions, and public favor or criticism. Through all the years the men of the Ranger service maintained a spirit among themselves and a reputation among others that became legend. The Texas Ranger organization was copied by some other western states and became known worldwide, both for the Rangers' actual activities and for the myths that grew up around them. Next to the Alamo and certain television programs, Rangers are the best-known element of the Texas legend.

The real Rangers stayed on, loyal to the law and devoted to the duty given them. The myths appeared in radio serials and movies, comic book epics, and tales so tall that there was no use in even trying to contradict them.

The Rangers served for many years directly under the governor of Texas and the adjutant general. In 1935 they became part of the Texas Department of Public Safety, and some of their functions were taken over by state highway patrolmen. Retained as a separate division of the department, Rangers assist police officers anywhere in the state, work on special assignments, and deal directly with major crime.

The majority of early Texas Rangers were, like the majority of people in Texas, of English heritage and often from the southern United States. Most were young. Many were farmers or cowboys who came West in search of excitement or escape. Quite a few were from other places in the world, with a wide variety of former occupations and education.

By far the next largest group, from private to captain, was Mexican in heritage. Many recruits were born in Mexico, generally in the northern states. Hundreds served, particularly along the Rio Grande border.

Indians also served as scouts and regular Rangers, but men of Native American heritage are difficult to total. For a long time, being "part Indian" was not exactly fashionable.

Although some enlistment papers are signed merely with an "X" – and give, perhaps deliberately, no further information about the individual – others list quite a few interesting former occupations and places of birth. In particular, many French and German men are on the rolls. Included are Parisian butchers; German surveyors, masons, and farmers; an Alsatian engineer; a Mexican vaquero; a French soldier; an English farmer born in London; a Swiss blacksmith; a Mexican bricklayer; an Ohio schoolteacher; a Prussian sailor; and a New York City clerk. At least one man simply listed his place of birth as "on the Ocean." There were printers and painters, laborers and mechanics, cattlemen and carpenters. Some individuals were hired, when necessary, as wagon masters or blacksmiths; most were enlisted. Thus, Ranger groups were mixed. They included Black teamsters and smiths, Germans and Mexicans who could speak little English, veterans of the French Foreign Legion, Englishmen "with education" and a few

Rangers Frank Hamer (left) and R.M. Hudson, photographed the day after they killed Ed Putnam at Del Rio, December 1, 1906

Look at that 6-foot ranger here on my right. I saw him receive the fire of a Comanche Indian at the distance of thirty paces, without dodging, and now [at a dinner in Decatur] he is so confused and scared he has just told that black-eyed girl he did not use coffee, and I have seen him sit down around a camp fire, and drink a level quart of it, strong and black, without sugar.

—A.J. Sowell

without, men who painted and wrote poetry in quiet hours after duty, amateur geologists, and former mercenaries. In 1988 the first Black, a veteran Department of Public Safety criminal intelligence investigator, was appointed to the regular service. In modern times one or two women were named as Special Rangers, but none to the regular service.

Groups of Rangers from the German settlements in Texas used German as their principal language, and more than one unit of Rangers consisted of almost all Mexicans (one such company had only two Anglo-Americans in a total of sixty men.

Before the Civil War a unit of Rangers who held still long enough to be counted contained eleven men from Tennessee; eight from Kentucky; six each from Alabama, Missouri, and Georgia; five from Germany; three each from Louisiana, Arkansas, and Illinois; two each from Ireland, Mexico, New York, and Virginia; one each from Scotland, North Carolina, New Hampshire, Ohio, Pennsylvania, and New Jersey—and three native Texans.

Such a mix was typical.

Capt. W.L. Barler of Texas Ranger Company E, an experienced border Ranger, alternatively served during Prohibition as a Mounted Customs River Rider for the United States Customs Service. When this photograph was taken on May 3, 1918, some eight miles from Del Rio, Capt. Barler was paid $125 a month in salary. Like all Rangers, he furnished horse, saddle, rifle, pistol, meals, and lodging. If a Ranger's horse died in action, the State did pay for a new one; if a Ranger was killed on the job, no one received any special payment.

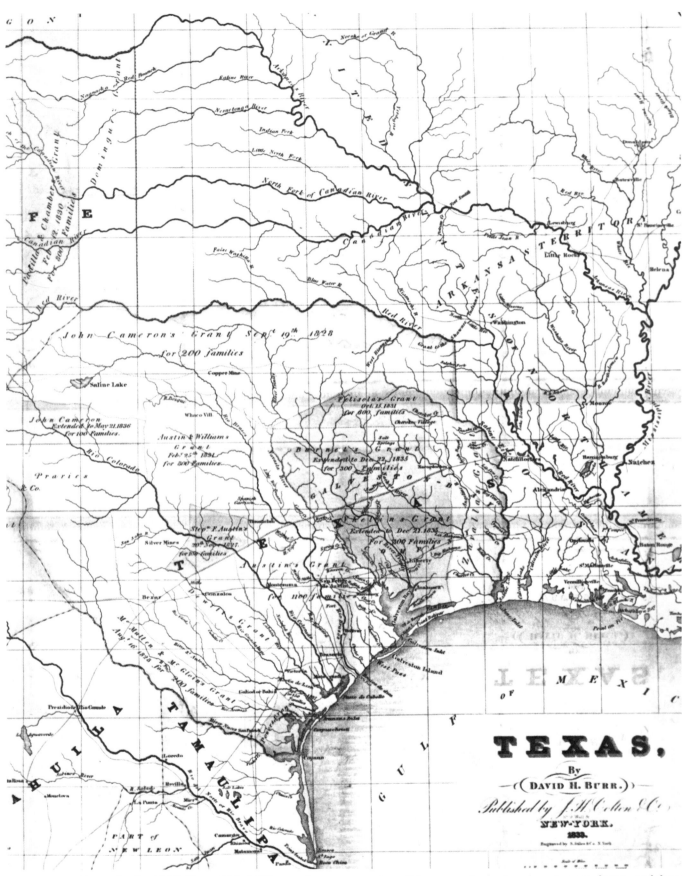

Texas by David H. Burr—This 1833 map shows one version of the many Anglo-American guesses, hopes, and fears concerning the borders of the Mexican province. On this map the Nueces is still the southern border, and land grants—actual and near-imaginary—fill most of the area.

I. COLONIAL TEXAS AND THE REPUBLIC

The Texas rangers were created in 1823 by Stephen F. Austin . . . and in 1832 by a General Convention of the Colonists . . . and in 1835 by a later revolutionary government . . . and by frontier needs in 1839. . . . The Rangers were "first" created at each of these times and in many following years, almost never with the modern name of "Texas Rangers."

The word "ranger" is a fairly old one in English, and its history clearly indicates the concept. In the sense of a row or line of fighters or hunters, "range" was used more than 700 years ago. By 1470 it had the modern sense of a movement over a wide area for a variety of purposes: chasing the French, hunting deer, or pursuing women. By the year 1818 the English poet John Keats, in his *Endymion*, could write "I've been a ranger in search of pleasure throughout every clime."

But it was as a title for a forest officer, specifically a keeper of the royal parks, that the word "ranger" came into English almost as it would later be used in Texas. In 1455 English parliamentary records noted the office of "Raungers of oure said Forestes." One of the duties of the office was the policing of rural areas. The term was used thereafter by English poets such as Dryden and novelists such as Scott. Ranging, in the sense of scouting and protecting

"Mounted gunmen, spies, and Rangers . . ."

In the Republic of Texas and during the early years of statehood, many companies of men were raised under a variety of names for the purpose of defending the frontier. They were enlisted for limited, brief terms—often from the areas where they were needed—and they usually provided their own horses and guns. In other words, they were Rangers. In 1840 they were called "volunteers" and "spies." In fact, "spy horses" were on one occasion furnished by the state.

In 1841 "volunteer companies" were raised, and in 1843 the word "militia" was used once for a temporary group of men, not part of the regular militia. Designated for frontier defense, they were placed under the command of the chief justice of the involved county.

John C. Hays in 1844 led "mounted gunmen"—certainly no euphemism—and in 1845 raised what were then called "detachments of troops." The latter, as expected, became United States troops in Mexico during the next three years.

The words "Rangers" or "Corps of Rangers" or "Ranging Companies" were used in the legal acts calling for irregular units for common defense; these were rarely used as formal titles. It was not until later years, for instance, in 1870 under Governor E.J. Davis, that the words "Texas Rangers" appeared in acts of the legislature.

property, was an English occupation for nearly 400 years before Anglo-Americans faced Native Americans in Central Texas.

In 18th century America rangers were necessary as Indian fighters in the more southern English colonies along the Atlantic coast. Records of the Georgia colony for 1733 note that a Captain Macpherson "with fifteen of the Rangers . . . protected the new Settlers." In 1742 it was claimed that "for the defense of the colony . . . it is necessary to have . . . rangers who can ride the woods."

And conflicts with Indians were as common in colonial Texas. They were, after all, losing their homelands to successive waves of well-armed newcomers. They rather naturally fought back—most often with quick raids by small groups of warriors—against the settlers. The targets were the settlers themselves and their children, cattle, and food. More rarely the Indians fought organized military units with large, allied groups of their own. The Spanish had countered raids with regular troops trained in frontier warfare and occasionally with armed vaqueros from large ranches. But the troops were too slow—and usually in the wrong place.

In Austin's first colony a mounted militia was permitted by the Mexican government, but the unit was insufficient to guard the frontier. Settlers had more pressing concerns—raising crops and building houses—than serving in a regular military force. Theoretically, Austin, as a militia officer, had forces in the field; actually, those forces were few. Some of the first were men led by John Tumlinson, an *alcalde* from the Colorado, and Josiah H. Bell from the Brazos. In 1823 Moses Morrison's company, in the field under Governor Trespalacios' authority, were rangers, although they did not go by that name.

Austin wanted to increase the protection given by the small militia and the few Mexican troops with highly mobile, well-armed rangers. He offered to ". . . employ ten men in addition to those employed by the government to act as rangers for the common defense. . . . The wages I will give the said ten men is fifteen dollars a month payable in property. . . ."

This was perhaps the first time the word "rangers" was used in Texas in this context. Austin's statement was written on the reverse of one of Land Commissioner Baron de Bastrop's proclamations to the colonists, dated August 5, 1823. But men, as well as pieces of paper, were scarce; the effort was unsuccessful. A permanent Ranger group was not formed.

When the Anglo-American colonists—as a convention, committee of safety, or full provisional government—faced the necessity of a ranging service, the appointments were temporary and not a part of a regular army or militia.

In October of 1832 representatives from the predominantly Anglo-American settlements met in a General Convention at San Felipe de Austin. To deal with sporadic Indian raids, this assembly suggested a separate "militia" from Austin's and DeWitt's colonies. These men differed from Rangers only in name.

As trouble with the Mexican government developed, local committees of safety and correspondence were formed. A "permanent council" of representatives from municipalities met in

October 1835. Many settlers saw a revolution as inevitable, but they had a number of troubles to consider. On October 17 Daniel Parker offered a resolution creating a Corps of Rangers intended to deal with Indians. One less problem would be welcome. "Superintendents" were to lead three groups: Silas Parker with 25 Rangers between the Brazos and Trinity rivers, Garrison Greenwood with ten Rangers on the east side of the Trinity, and D.B. Fryar with 25 between the Brazos and the Colorado. The pay was $1.25 a day. The Rangers elected their own officers, under the superintendents, and their duty was "to range and guard the frontiers" — whenever the officers thought necessary.

Scene near Austin, c. 1840

By November 13, 1835, the ordinance "establishing a provisional government" included as part of that government, in Article XXI, a "corps of rangers under the command of a major, to consist of one hundred and fifty men." This "battalion" was placed under the regular military commander.

A separate ordinance, passed just eleven days later, slightly redefined the group. The prerevolutionary General Council of Texas, meeting at San Felipe de Austin, passed an ordinance on November 24 which was, to that time, the most coherent and permanent-sounding order establishing the Texas Rangers. In addition to receiving capital letters, the new "Corps of Rangers" was kept apart from the regular army under its own leader. To be sure, it was ultimately under the commander-in-chief of the regular army, but this was paper authority. A "major" separately headed the force, making the Rangers autonomous.

They were now as well defined as they would be for the next forty years. In all significant respects, units of Rangers acted as

separate commands. Their instructions and orders came from immediate officers either appointed or elected by the Rangers themselves. The major did coordinate Ranger activities and could head a group himself, but, in times of immediate trouble, the local captain was final authority.

This was the force, led by Major R.M. "Three-Legged Willie" Williamson, which ranged between the retreating Texan army and the advancing Mexican troops during the 1836 revolution and after the fall of the Alamo. The Rangers aided settlers in fleeing the approaching enemy in the "Runaway Scrape" and served as the army's rear guard. They scouted for General Sam Houston, and at San Jacinto many served individually in various companies of the army.

Thus, by this date, many Ranger characteristics were obvious. The service was an irregular, paramilitary organization with largely self-defined limits of activity and officers. Rangers were given a blank check (in most regards except money) to do what was necessary to guard the frontier.

Coleman's Fort

Early Rangers, always in small, mobile groups, operated miles away from any headquarters and were responsible for scores of "camps" and "forts" along the Texas frontier. Many of these outposts were only temporary; others were blockhouses with wood stockades also used by local settlers, sometimes long after the Rangers moved farther west. At these camps and forts, the Rangers would gather at specified times, rest between scouts, store provisions, and occasionally take refuge.

Among the forts, a term which usually implied at least a stockade and cabin, if not a blockhouse, were Fort Colorado, or Coleman's Fort, established in 1836 east of Austin and Fort Fisher at Waco in 1837.

For speed in attack or retreat, and to cover the long Texas frontier, the Ranger worked on horseback. At first, his single-shot firearms were only useful, except as clubs, from the ground. All early battles were fought on foot, no matter how fast the horseman arrived. And, until the new weapons of the 1840's were available, the Indians had the advantage. A mounted Indian could discharge many arrows before a rifleman on the ground could reload — and the rifleman could not reload at all on horseback at a gallop. With the coming of a reliable repeating pistol, the situation was reversed. Rangers learned to fight from horseback at deadly speed.

always ready for active service, a good and sufficient horse, properly accoutred and equipped with saddle, bridle and blanket, at their own expense: and in default thereof, the captain or commanding officer of the said company to which said private belongs, shall cause a horse to be purchased for said private and charge him with the same, in the settlement of his quarterly accounts.

SEC. 3. **Be it further ordained and decreed, Et.,** that the officer in the said Corps, in addition to the per diem compensation of the privates in the Corps of Rangers, shall receive the same pay as the officers of the same rank and grade in the Regiment of Dragoons in the Army of the United States of America.

Passed at San Felipe de Austin, Nov. 24, 1835.

(Signed) JAMES W. ROBINSON,
Lieut. Gov. and ex-officio Pres't of G.C.

P.B. DEXTER,
Sec'y of the Gen. Council.

Approved, Nov. 26, 1835

HENRY SMITH,
Governor

CHARLES B. STEWART,
Executive Secretary

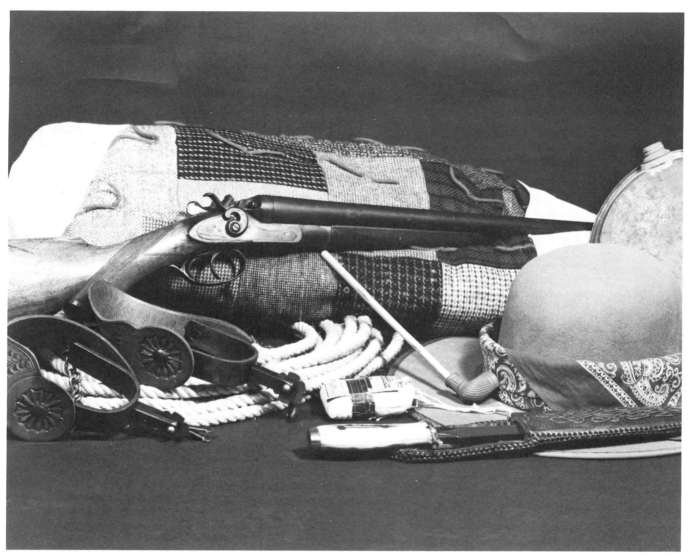

Typical Ranger's gear

In addition to rifle, pistol, and knife, the Ranger carried the same items as the cowboy or trail rider: blankets, leather and cloth wallets for salt and ammunition, parched corn spiced or sweetened to alleviate thirst, dried meat, tobacco, canteen, rope, and — sometimes — a gum rubber raincoat. He provided his own equipment. For the rest, he lived off the land. At times living off the land created problems. The *Telegraph and Texas Register* reported that where the land was thinly sprinkled with settlers, a new complaint was heard. Before the Rangers came — so the settlers said — Indians killed their children; after the Rangers moved in — so the settlers claimed — someone killed their hogs.

In 1836 the pay for these "mounted riflemen now and hereafter in the ranging service on the frontier" was set at $25 a month. Officers received up to $75 a month. They all drew the same land bounty as regular military men, one of the strong inducements to newcomers. Few native Texans were among the earlier Rangers, for obvious reasons. Some arrivals probably took the job simply because it was available and because it was a good way to learn about the new country.

Cylinder engraving prepared for the Colt Dragoon. The fanciful design (as far as uniforms and dress go) takes inspiration from such victories as Jack Hays managed against Indians in Texas when he and his Rangers were armed with the first repeating five-shooters. For the first time, traditional Indian weaponry was no match for guns.

Rangers had a short term of enlistment, three to six months at first and rarely longer than a year, but many individuals served more than one term. The organization was simple. Natural leaders emerged from the ranks and were accepted as officers. And the officer literally led his men—he did not simply tell them what to do. In any case, the Rangers were to defend their territory according to their own rules, as long as they were within the broad scope of frontier justice. If they wished, their territory could take the horizon as a boundary. And, in such a place, frontier justice did not require a courtroom trial.

Always numerically few, Rangers learned to strike hard and fast, often adopting the fighting tactics and ground of the enemy. And, from their first enemies, the Indians, they learned a lot.

When the ranging companies were first organized, Captain Tumlinson's company on the Colorado included Noah Smithwick, who would write one of the most interesting of the histories of Texas. He included a typical early-Ranger incident:

In January of 1836 Smithwick was near the future site of Austin. The town was not there, but the earliest Anglo-American settlers were, and some sixty Rangers met to build a frontier post. The 1836 revolution had effectively started the previous December, but frontier defense was no less important.

Near suppertime a young woman dragged herself into the Ranger camp, exhausted. Her clothes were in shreds, torn in her escape from Indians the day before. Mrs. Hibbons's story was not uncommon. When attacked by Comanches, she was traveling with her husband, brother, and two small children to the Guadalupe River, where they hoped to establish a home. The Indians—skilled mounted warriors—still controlled much of the land. The two men and her older child were all killed, and she and the baby were captured.

My plan always was, when there was a momentous job on hand, to go right at it and get it over with.

—Noah Smithwick

15

Robert McAlpin Williamson had been crippled by polio in childhood. His right leg was bent back at the knee, and he wore a peg leg from the knee down, giving him the imposed nickname "Three-Legged-Willie." Neither nickname nor wooden leg slowed him down. He danced a lively jig and played a wicked banjo at many a frontier party.

A firebrand editor and brilliant lawyer, Williamson came to Texas from Georgia and became known as the "Patrick Henry of the Texas Revolution." The editorials and orations he added to the revolutionary cause soon obliged the Mexican government to put a price on his head.

The Indians camped near the future site of Austin on the Colorado River and, sheltered by a thick stand of cedar, bedded down in the teeth of a norther. Mrs. Hibbons left the child to their mercy and escaped in the cold, wind-torn night. She knew that another day's travel northwest would take her much too far away from any settlements. After a long walk downriver through icy water, brush, and briers, she found the Ranger camp late the next afternoon.

The Rangers broke camp immediately, but after some distance, and afraid of losing the trail in the dark, they halted until morning. At first light they were back on the trail; they caught up with the Indians at mid-morning and attacked. In the short fight the child was rescued, one Indian was killed, and the others fled upriver.

⭐　　⭐　　⭐

Almost all of the time, Rangers provided their own equipment, but in 1837 those at Coleman's Fort near Austin received clothing from an unexpected source: army surplus. After the Texan victory at San Jacinto in April of 1836, the newly organized government of the Republic of Texas made a few coherent attempts to supply its army. Rangers received the leftovers.

Smithwick noted that the government sent army clothing, "pantaloons and runabouts," but all the wrong size. The Rangers divided them purely by lot and made do with what they received. The arrangement produced much laughter.

One man, Wolfenberger, was left with pants that barely made it below his knees and a jacket which failed to reach his belt by a good six inches—but Wolfenberger was a quick man with thread and needle. He soon pieced out the clothes with blanket strips.

⭐　　⭐　　⭐

An interesting group of Rangers in the early days of the republic was a unit under Isaac W. Burton which earned the title of "horse marines."

Burton, a Ranger captain since 1835, was given the job of patrolling the Texas coast in 1836 after the battle of San Jacinto. Mexico by no means recognized the Republic of Texas, so the Texans feared a Mexican landing by sea.

The Rangers did sight a vessel June 3 in Copano Bay. Burton's men concealed themselves while one signaled the ship. A number of sailors, rowing ashore in a small boat, were quickly captured. Sixteen Rangers then took the boat and rowed back out. Apparently mistaken at first for friends, they captured the *Watchman* lying offshore with supplies for the Mexican army. But, before the Rangers could leave the bay with the captured vessel, two other ships, the *Comanche* and the *Fanny Butler*, came up. They also were in Mexican service.

The Rangers forced the captain of the *Watchman* to decoy the officers of the other two ships aboard. They captured them and soon were in command of all three ships, loaded with a net haul of $25,000 in supplies. These were turned over to the regular army at Velasco, ending one of the few amphibious operations of the Texas Rangers.

For several years after 1836, the Centralists of Mexico had too many troubles to put any further military force in Texas. Alleged efforts to incite the Indians against Texas settlers and conflicts between the Anglo-Americans on the expanding frontier and the Indians themselves kept the Rangers busy.

On January 15, 1839, the government of the Republic of Texas passed an act again renewing the ranging service and calling for a company of 56 men. The duration was for three months at a total cost of $5,000. Their duty was "to range on the frontier of Gonzales County and protect the settlements."

Battle of Plum Creek

Specific provisions like this were never enough. A few days later a Corps of Rangers was created: two companies of 56 men to protect San Patricio, Goliad, and Refugio counties for six months. The total expense was to be $15,000. As usual, most equipment, arms, and horses were furnished by the individual Rangers. As usual, other groups were raised as needed, sometimes without clear provision for pay. And, as usual, the Ranger service was supported by a patchwork of government acts, but all for the same reasons.

In the days of the republic, fights with Indians occurred over much of Central Texas, often near rivers, large and small, which gave their names to battles: the Sabine, Brazos, Colorado, San Gabriel, Llano, Little River, and Walnut Creek. The bodies of Indians and Rangers also fell among nameless ravines and hills laced with prairie flowers.

Those who fought the native Indians in these years were not only Rangers. Volunteer groups—as they were frequently called—were often a mix of Texas militia, Rangers, Indian scouts and allies, and actual volunteers—very temporary enlistees from the new settlements threatened by Indian attack.

Colonel John H. Moore, leading a volunteer unit in October of 1840, surprised a group of Comanches—some sixty families and over a hundred warriors—camped in a bend of the upper Colorado. As morning broke, the Rangers and others, who (like the Indians) had spent the night in the grip of icy weather, shook off the cold and dashed into the encampment. They fired in all directions. Some Indians were driven into the cold water to

In November of 1835, when the more formal Corps of Rangers was established, Williamson was chosen leader, the first major in the service. Five months later he joined Smith's Cavalry for the San Jacinto battle, dashing up at the last minute to join the fight. He had been in the field for weeks. His hair was long, his beard matted and tangled. He wore a suit of dirty buckskin, stained and stiff from sweat and cold spring rains. On his head was a fur cap with nine coontails dangling to his shoulders. Other men with him that day said later that some of the enemy who encountered him simply died of fright.

Williamson later became a district judge, member of the Texas Supreme Court, and legislator.

In the summer of 1840, Comanche Indians—and allies—raided down the Guadalupe River valley in retribution for the Council House fight in San Antonio some five months earlier. The Indians considered the San Antonio fight a treacherous breach of honor on the part of the Republic of Texas and took revenge by looting, killing, and burning settlements on their way southeast.

On their return they were met by a volunteer army at Plum Creek near present Lockhart. Included in this force that defeated the Comanches on August 11 were Rangers led by Ben McCulloch.

Charles de Montel, a native of Königsberg, Germany, was one of the men to captain a company of the Frontier Regiment, Mounted Rangers, during the first years of the Civil War.

De Montel had come to Texas in 1836, served in Houston's army, and later worked as a surveyor and guide. For Henri Castro he led the original colonists to Castroville and himself became a founder of the Alsatian town. In 1853 he surveyed the Bandera townsite and helped settle Polish colonists in the area. As a Ranger de Montel was captain of Company G for Bandera, Blanco, Medina, and Uvalde counties.

After this service he commanded the steamer Texas, *a private vessel in Confederate assignment.*

drown; others awoke only to die by gunfire. Survivors were pursued on horseback beyond the river for several miles.

In full daylight Moore observed what, to the Texans, was payment for years of Indian raids against isolated settlers: the "bodies of men, women, and children . . . on every hand wounded, dying, and dead." By midmorning the Indian camp was a sheet of ashes blowing in the sharp wind.

Less fortunate, from the Ranger viewpoint, was Captain John Bird, who, in May of the previous year, was surprised by Indians near present Marlin in Falls County. His Rangers, 35 in number, gave chase to a small group of Indians but, unable to close the distance between them, abandoned the chase. As they turned away the Rangers found themselves surrounded — in a trap.

Taking cover in a ravine, they were soon facing some 200 Indians, well-mounted, armed, and angry. The first charge of Indians was beaten off — not a second. Seven Rangers, including Captain Bird, were dead when night put an end to the battle. As darkness fell the Indians gave up the attack. Nathan Brookshire, who had assumed command, reported a strange sight in the gathering dusk. As the Indians rode away, some threw "up in the air a composition of something that had the appearance of lightning," and their voices filled the darkness with wails for their own dead.

From such conflicts emerged renowned Ranger leaders such as Ben McCulloch and Jack Hays. Hate and respect also evolved — on both sides.

Traditions were quick to form. A Ranger leader had to have the support of his men. He was often elected by them. The Rangers also had their own form of discipline — very little — but of a type adapted to trail life, not to a military campaign. When Captain William Eastland succeeded Captain Andrews, he attempted to exercise a more military type of discipline. Without a long delay the Rangers decided, and said, that they would go home and Eastland could go to hell. Eastland gracefully and quickly yielded, and the Rangers stayed between the thin line of settlement and the Indians.

San Antonio always needed a military force. After the 1836 revolution the Mexican government could not maintain a conquering army in Texas but could, and did, march in with punitive expeditions. San Antonio de Béxar was continually threatened by Mexican invasion and was, in the days of the republic, very much on the Indian frontier.

John Coffee "Jack" Hays was 21 when he came to San Antonio about 1837. He may have been in Ranger service earlier under Deaf Smith or Henry W. Karnes. Hays was a surveyor and a natural leader who was named a Ranger captain in 1840 to guard the San Antonio area, to the south and west, in the absence of regular troops — a commission he held until after the Mexican War.

In the years of the republic, a new opponent was added to the Ranger list: the Mexican bandit, invader, or troublemaker — as defined by Anglo law.

John Coffee "Jack" Hays. The name given to Hays by the Comanches—man-it-is-very-bad-luck-to-get-in-fight-with-because-devils-help-him—was one word in the Indian language. It was shortened by the Europeans who knew it to "Devil Jack."

South of San Antonio stretched trade routes traveled by Anglo-American and Mexican merchants across land claimed by both Texas and Mexico: the brush country between the Nueces River and the Rio Grande. Traders found the routes profitable whether or not Mexico and Texas were officially at war, but bandits were a real problem. When traders were attacked early in 1841 by Mexican freebooters, Hays rode south from San Antonio with Captain Antonio Pérez. With the two captains were 25 rangers: 12 were Anglo-American in heritage; 13 were Mexican. Not one was in a mood to respect boundaries.

About ten miles from Laredo, Captain García of the Mexican army and 35 troopers rode out to oppose them. Hays and Pérez's presence in the area was considered an invasion by the Mexicans, simply a pursuit of bandits by Hays. Suspecting that the bandits had taken refuge in Laredo, Hays and Pérez charged the Mexican troops and, in two engagements, routed them.

1836 Colt Patterson

The Texan unit then proceeded to Laredo, which was surrendered by the *alcalde*. It was a surprising conclusion to a Ranger pursuit. Not surprising, so far from their base, was the abandonment of the town shortly thereafter by Hays and Pérez; no effort was made there to formally establish Republic of Texas sway. After annexation the United States flag was raised over the city at the time of the Mexican War, and the man who hoisted it then was a Texas Ranger: Addison Gillespie.

But, in the early 1840's, the Republic of Texas, in deep debt, could not keep an army in the field at San Antonio. Organized forces there were disbanded except for the "few spies under Captain John C. Hays." San Antonio was thus taken twice by Mexican armies, but they returned to Mexico, each time followed by Hays. He did not have sufficient strength to mount significant attacks, yet did cause enough damage to rate a $500 price on his head.

Hays was more effective against the Indians, setting a pace that established him as a legendary Ranger leader. The Indian chief Flacco, a friend of Captain Jack, called him "bravo too much."

In 1841 Hays and a few Rangers escorted a surveying party into the Central Texas Hill Country north of present-day Fredericksburg. One evening the group camped just south of Enchanted Rock, a granite mountain long considered sacred by the Indians — and thereafter a theme even in Anglo stories. Indians were thought to conduct strange rites on the summit; spirit lights and weird sounds were said to play along the slopes of the bare rock, and ghostly warriors supposedly frequented a mysterious cave

near the top. Here was a place of lucrative but lost mines, wandering and treacherous wraiths, and outrageous forms of human sacrifice. Most of the stories are invention. But, whatever the stories, the mountain provides beautiful views from its top—which were probably what Jack Hays was seeking when, rising early, he climbed the granite dome alone in a brilliant morning sunrise.

Hays, of course, had strapped on his heavy Colt revolvers, saying, within Ben McCulloch's hearing, "I may not need you, but if I do, I will need you mighty bad." He did. Comanche warriors had been tracking the party and, on the morning of Hays's walk, recognized him as he left camp. They decided to surround their old enemy on the dome and butcher him. They attacked, but Hays made it to the top, where weathered, broken rock gave him good cover. Hays's repeating pistols took a fearful toll of Indians before his men, following the sounds of battle, arrived and drove the attackers from the slopes.

On June 8, 1844, Hays and 14 other Rangers carried off a similar victory by routing some eighty Comanches on the Pedernales River north of San Antonio. The Rangers were armed with the new five-shooters, while the Indians had expected the tactics of Rangers armed with single-shot weapons.

Early battle tactics called for the Rangers to ride to an engagement with rifle, shotgun, and pistol: all single-shot weapons and none suitable from horseback. Shooting was done as alternately as possible, some men reloading while others fired, all dismounted. "An Indian could discharge a dozen arrows while a man was

The Rangers were Indian exterminators; the soldiers were only guards.

—Walter Prescott Webb

Oversized William Alexander Wallace was a descendant of the Scots William Wallace and Robert Bruce, who maintained Scottish independence against England in the late 13th century. Bruce, by 1313, was perhaps the most renowned Scots warrior and king. The later Wallace was of similar temperament. He came from Virginia to Texas to "take pay out of the Mexicans" for a brother and a cousin killed at Goliad in the midst of the 1836 revolution.

He fought Mexican troops led into Texas by General Woll and invaded Mexico itself as a member of the Mier Expedition, which ended in disaster and capture. When released from Perote Prison, he returned to Texas—but not for long. He joined Captain Jack Hays's Rangers, then returned south for the Mexican War.

In the 1850's Wallace led a Ranger company of his own and during the Civil War stayed on the Texas frontier to guard against Indian attack.

He was as resourceful as he was brave. Once, returning from a lone scout, he emerged from a thicket to find himself face to face with a war party of 30 Comanches. His horse was in no shape for a quick escape, but Wallace was.

"Come on, boys! Here they are!" Wallace rose in his stirrups, yelling and waving over his shoulder to the empty woods behind him. The Indians may not have understood the language, but the gesture left no doubt. They took to the brush.

loading a gun," Noah Smithwick observed, "and if they could manage to draw our fire all at once, they had us at their mercy unless we had a safe retreat."

The Indians tried such strategy against Hays. The Rangers fired a broadside, and the Indians charged, confident that they had time to engage the Rangers at close range. But each Ranger had four shots to go—from each pistol. They used them. This victory for the repeating weapon was so decisive and sudden that the battle was used later as an engraving on some Colt revolver cylinders. The scene, somewhat heroically depicted, was designed by a participant, Samuel Walker.

The Rangers became deadly marksmen from horseback and apparently influenced the tactics of the United States Cavalry during the Mexican War and for years to come.

San Antonio was an unlikely place for Comanches and Texas Rangers to meet under any circumstances. In 1843, however, they met there for a peaceful riding match rather than for a fight. Many city residents came out to see and compete in the show, held on a prairie a mile west of "downtown." The contest was promised to "beat a circus all hollow."

The Rangers were dressed in their best. For many this meant buckskin hunting shirts, leggings, and slouched hats, with braces of pistols and bowie knives stuck in their belts. Before the events a few of them had charged, horses and all, into a barroom, calling for mescal and red-eye. The diversion apparently did not increase their skills.

The Comanche riders, with natural dignity, sat like bright statues waiting for the contest. Their feathers, furs, and face paint added color to the dusty scene.

Mexican caballeros of the city rode proudly to the field on fiery mustangs, wearing big sombreros, bright scarves, and slashed trousers.

The activities soon began, with each rider—at full gallop—picking up a spear from flat on the ground. A glove was then substituted for the spear. Then a target replaced the glove—the Indians shooting two arrows at full speed, Rangers and caballeros a like number of bullets. The riders next demonstrated trick-riding techniques and modes of attack and defense. The last activity of the day was horse breaking.

A young man from Florida, McMullen, won first prize of the day, with the next three places going to Long Quiet, a Comanche; Colonel Kinney of Corpus Christi; and Don Rafael, a ranchero from near the Rio Grande.

In spite of such pleasant afternoons, San Antonio in the early 1840's was a rough place. Not far out of town to the west were open lands the Comanches had taken from Apaches. Anglos regarded San Antonio as the most westward pioneer settlement in Texas, even though it was nowhere near the vague western border of the land taken from Mexico. Neither Mexico nor Spain had considered the settlement much more than a frontier. Now, to

William Alexander Wallace

When the sound of Comanche hoofbeats had become silence, Wallace rode on alone through the clearing back to camp.

"Bigfoot," as he came to be known, was a frontiersman, tale teller, stage driver, and fighter—and one source for the "larger-than-life" Texan myth. Back in Virginia on visits, he found that people accepted great lies and great truth on a fairly equal basis. He rarely passed up an opportunity to tell a story; the story was rarely less than hair-raising.

In the Texas State Cemetery at Austin, a small stone gives the simple truth: "Here lies he who spent his manhood defending the homes of Texans."

San Antonio de Béxar, c. 1850

The government didn't furnish feed for the horses nor to any extent for the men, either.

— Noah Smithwick

such a place came new businesses, faiths, and lives. Rangers were often employed as escorts to and from San Antonio.

In 1844 John Wesley DeVilbiss and John McCullough brought Methodism and Presbyterianism, respectively, to San Antonio. Surveying the area, they were escorted from Seguin by several of Jack Hays's Rangers, who later became friends – after a slight misunderstanding – with the Methodist.

DeVilbiss, assigned to San Antonio in 1846, ran into two spots of trouble while conducting worship services at a temporary location: the old government building used as a courthouse on the west plaza. The first problem was cockfighting held in the plaza, apparently always during church services. The second problem concerned the Rangers themselves. The minister, after observing Rangers when he had first traveled to San Antonio, and perhaps subsequently, published a friendly criticism of their character in the *Western Christian Advocate*. Some of the Rangers were wide readers. They took his words in a similar lighthearted manner, letting it be known that they would duck him in the San Antonio River their next free afternoon.

DeVilbiss heard of their threat and, in true frontier spirit, invited them over for an explanation of what he had said. Some of the Rangers did drop by to listen before carrying out their resolve. Apparently appeased, they did not throw the pastor in the river. A couple of them even stayed on as regular congregation members. Strangely enough, cockfighting disappeared from the plaza until worship services moved elsewhere.

A CHICKEN FIGHTER.

25

TEXAS RANGER
Mexican War
1846

A Ranger during the Mexican War, 1846

II. EARLY STATEHOOD
AND THE MEXICAN WAR

In July of 1845 General Zachary Taylor, commanding United States forces, arrived at the mouth of the Nueces River. Texas was negotiating annexation with the United States, and the United States was ready to go to war with Mexico to defend Texas' claim to the Rio Grande as its southern boundary. If all of Texas was not disputed land, certainly the land between the Nueces and the Rio Grande was.

The tempo of the political dance quickened. The United States, committed to the annexation of Texas, had military forces in the disputed republic well before formal annexation on December 29, 1845. Texas' last president, Anson Jones, continued in office until February 19, 1846, when the Lone Star flag – as the flag of a republic – was lowered and J. Pinckney Henderson was inaugurated as first governor of the 28th U.S. state. General Taylor had been told as early as October of 1845 by Secretary of War W.L. Marcy that "Texas is now fully incorporated into our union." Marcy added, a bit early, that Taylor should "make a requisition upon the executive of that State for such of its militia force as may be needed to repel invasion. . . ." In fact, the U.S. was planning to do the invading, and the first Texas soldiers – who cared little for exact dates or niceties of diplomatic language – were Rangers under Captain Samuel Walker.

One of the toughest fighting men of the Mexican War earned his ominous nickname through an act of formal courtesy. As adjutant for Hays's Rangers, Colonel John Salmon Ford notified the families of men killed in action. His normal "Rest in Peace," an ending for most of his letters, changed to a brief "R.I.P." under battle conditions. For the rest of his life, he was known as "Rip" Ford.

The native of South Carolina was a man of many talents. He was a doctor, lawyer, surveyor, newspaperman, soldier, and politician. He and Robert Neighbors blazed an immigrant trail from San Antonio to El Paso in 1849, and later he was captain of a company of Texas Rangers in South Texas just north of the Rio Grande.

During the Civil War he was a Confederate cavalry commander and participated in the last battle of the war, Palmito Ranch in the Lower Rio Grande Valley. He then served two terms in the Texas Senate before spending his last days writing his memoirs.

Ultimately, what was at stake was the entire northern area of Mexico, which included future western Texas, New Mexico, Arizona, California, and parts of Utah, Colorado, and Nevada. The northern boundary of New Spain and Mexico had never really been agreed on, as the area was not well defined, but the United States wanted most of it. The claims of the Republic of Texas were a wonderful excuse.

And there were private grievances. Men like Walker, a fiery, natural commander, had suffered at Mexican hands during an ill-fated Texas invasion of Mexico. He and others were ready to fight. Texans alone could not put a significant army in the field, but, as part of the United States Army, they had precisely what they wanted: a chance to fight Mexico on favorable terms and on Mexican soil.

The Rangers were among the most eager.

Ben McCulloch and Rangers during the Mexican War, 1846

General Taylor soon mustered several companies of Rangers into the national service. The men were known as "Texas Rangers," although not mustered in with that name. In theory, they served under Texas Governor J. Pinckney Henderson but were in federal service as the 1st and 2nd Regiments of Texas Mounted Volunteers. Immediate commanders were Colonels Jack Hays from San Antonio and George T. Wood of the "East Texas Rangers." Other leaders quickly became obvious. Ben McCulloch made a name for himself as a scout in the advance of the army in northern Mexico. General Taylor, in moving south, asked for two companies of Rangers to act as scouts and to keep communication lines open, in relief of the regular cavalry. What he got were men who fought with a bloody ferocity in the forefront of many battles in the Mexican War – "Los Diablos Tejanos."

The "devils" were not all ruffians. Doctors, lawyers, poets, surveyors, and legislators were in the ranks. Greek and Latin writers were occasionally quoted around the campfires. But these men managed to look rougher and dirtier than modern movie desper-

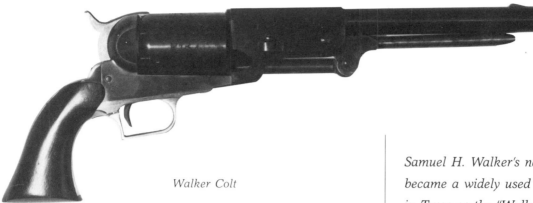

Walker Colt

adoes, were armed like a cliché to the teeth, and had no reservations about killing.

And they were soon involved in the more interesting atrocities of the conflict. One of the most flagrant was the "incident" at Hacienda San Francisco de los Patos in Coahuila. To some people, the story is absolute truth; to others, it is fiction.

As the most exciting version goes, a unit of Rangers was acting as escort for a group of United States supply wagons on the way south. The road was long and not entirely exciting. One evening the Rangers camped by a large hacienda. Nearby at least one of the Rangers found a cantina. It is a familiar episode. After a heroic number of late-afternoon drinks, and, since the locale offered few diversions, the Ranger decided to desecrate the local church. He ripped down the huge altar crucifix and dragged it behind his horse as he departed the plaza. When an elderly priest gave chase and attempted to grab the crucifix, the Ranger turned and rode him down.

Local residents, however, were watching. Dragging a cross in the dirt was one thing, but trampling a priest was another. They

Texas Rangers in federal service meet Mexican lancers during the Mexican War, 1846.

Samuel H. Walker's name became a widely used word in Texas as the "Walker Colt" became the revolutionary handgun that altered the style of frontier fighting.

Born in Maryland, Walker came to Texas after establishing a reputation for courage and coolness during Indian battles in the southeastern United States. He was a member of Jack Hays's Rangers but spent much of his time in New York dealing with Samuel Colt in the purchase of arms for the Republic of Texas. His suggestions for changes in the Colt guns resulted in the popular Walker Colt models, which became common wherever there were Rangers, cowboys, or frontiersmen.

In 1842 Walker joined the Mier Expedition, was captured, and ended up in a Mexican prison. On his release he vowed to return to Mexico—but not as a prisoner. He did. As a member of the United States Mounted Rifles, he fought at Monterrey and later on the road to Mexico City. Walker was killed during the last engagements of the war.

surrounded the rider and pulled him to the ground. The Ranger was tied to a hastily built cross – in one version, the very cross he had pulled from the church – and was quite slowly flayed alive.

His horse, in the manner of later movies, escaped and returned to camp. Searching for him, the entire troop of Rangers rode back just as a beautiful sunset illuminated the screaming Ranger, dying and stripped of his skin by his torturers. The Rangers attacked, leaving most of the Mexicans dead around the body of their comrade, whom they themselves shot rather than allow him to suffer.

The hacienda owner had the nerve to bring the story to the attention of the United States Army commander, the Rangers told a story of justifiable retribution, and the army decided to keep the affair secret.

Or so the story goes – one among many.

Ben McCulloch and Ranger scouts taking stock of a Mexican army camp, February 1847

The Mexican War was pursued on two fronts, as far as the Texas Rangers were concerned: the advance to Monterrey with General Taylor and the capture of Mexico City by General Scott. In both cases, they were detailed to scout duty for the army and assigned to keep the rear line of march free of guerrillas. They did more.

At Monterrey the Rangers were soon involved in major conflicts. They composed half of the United States forces that captured "Independence Hill" overlooking the city. Except for Hays's battle with Colonel Juan N. Najera's cavalry, the Texans at Monterrey fought as infantry assault troops.

30

Sam Walker's charge at Huamantla, Mexico, October 9, 1847, during the Mexican War

The Rangers excelled, but, under siege conditions or between battles, even on some scouts, they were trouble. General Taylor could not manage them after the capture of Monterrey, and some Rangers were discharged. He wrote that "the mounted men from Texas have scarcely made one expedition without unwarrantably killing a Mexican. . . . There is scarcely a form of crime that has not been reported to me as committed by them. . . ." But the regular army continued to use Rangers in practically every conflict. And the Rangers were most willing: during the war there were some 1,300 enlistments.

To the south, on the road between Veracruz and Mexico City, General Scott's communications line was thin. He was harassed by a guerrilla operation on the part of the Mexicans even as their regular army crumbled in front of him.

Jack Hays arrived in 1847 to help clear the road for Scott. He brought 500 new Colt six-shooters for his men.

Gradually the Rangers' side of the war took on the characteristics of guerrilla combat. The Rangers not only kept the roads open, but also pursued the Mexicans into their mountain retreats. They took few prisoners and their reputation grew.

Their appearance, certainly intentional, always caused comment. At Puebla Albert Brackett of the Indiana Volunteers, a regular army man, noted that the Rangers were "an odd-looking set of fellows, and it seems to be their aim to dress as outlandishly as possible. Bob-tailed coats and "long-tailed blues," low and high-crowned hats, some slouched and others Panama, with a sprin-

"Texas has done more for me & my armes then all the country besides they have a better knowledge of ther use & want every texan ranger in Mexico to be thus armed before they are furnished any other troops."

– Samuel Colt to
Sam Houston, 1847

31

When Ben McCulloch resigned from the Texas legislature in 1846 to organize a Ranger company for service in the Mexican War, he had no trouble finding recruits. He had an established reputation as frontiersman and fighter not diminished by a crippled arm earned in an earlier duel with rifles. He had manned one of the Twin Sister cannons at San Jacinto and followed this with several years of expeditions against Indians.

McCulloch's main fame as a Ranger came from his service as scout and spy for the army of General Taylor. He distinguished himself in legendary penetrations of enemy lines and long advance scouts to determine the best routes for the regulars.

After the war McCulloch went to California, where, as Sacramento County sheriff, he stayed out of the gold rush. Back in Texas, he was

kling of black leather caps . . . and [a] thorough coating of dust over all . . . their huge beards gave them a savage appearance. Each man carried a rifle, a pair of pistols and . . . two of Colt's revolvers[;] a hundred of them could discharge a thousand shots in two minutes." There was no difference in dress between officers and men.

Another observer, Lieutenant Colonel Ebenezer Dumont, described mounted Rangers: "They rode, some standing upright, some sideways, some by the reverse flank, some faced to the rear, some on horses, some on asses, some on mustangs, and some on mules." Some were showing off.

Contemporary painting by Bruce Marshall of Rangers in Puebla, Mexico, in 1847, taken from descriptions written by Albert Brackett of the Indiana Volunteers, U.S. Army, and Lt. Col. Ebenezer Dumont

The Rangers were known and feared in Mexico City, yet many Mexicans lined the streets of their occupied city to look at the Texas devils as they entered. The day was not without incident. At least twice a rock was thrown at the Texans; at least twice a Mexican fell, dead from a Colt revolver.

Newspaper reports commented that Hays's men were in fact disciplined — but only in their own way. Disciplined or not, the Rangers were fond of "retaliation." One morning eighty Mexicans lay dead in the streets, not the result of organized battle.

After this, General Scott found duty for them outside the city. Once they almost captured Santa Anna, and they were with General Jo Lane in a guerrilla battle at Sequaltepan on February 25, 1848, probably the last conflict of the war.

Santa Anna asked permission to leave the country. The request was granted by both Mexico and the United States. At one point on his journey to the coast, he passed silent files of Rangers, who had been told by Jack Hays not to make a move. They did not.

At the war's end the Rangers were mustered out at Veracruz.

During the Mexican War the Texas frontier was not quiet. Most of the federal troops were on the war fronts in Mexico, and most

Treasury warrant of the Republic of Texas issued to John C. Hays on January 22, 1844

Rangers had enlisted. Some Indians and a few bandits found the times quite congenial.

In June of 1846 Colonel William S. Harney asked for five companies of mounted Rangers to enter the federal service but to stay in Texas as frontier defense. They were called for a term of six months under Captains John H. Conner at Castroville, John J. Grumbles at San Antonio, S. P. Ross on Little River, T. J. Smith on the Brazos near Waco, and Andrew Stapp on the west fork of the Trinity.

A wrangle ensued about mustering them into federal service, and, in the meantime, they were not paid. At first, only three companies were raised. Frontier protection was thin in the early days of Texas' statehood.

Governor J.P. Henderson returned from Mexico and took over the frontier problem, among others, from Acting Governor Horton. He asked Hays to go to Washington to convince Congress of the importance of frontier defense in Texas. Hays did, and more frontier units were raised, yet most were sent to Mexico, leaving only a few organized men in Texas. After the Mexican War the need for Rangers to oppose either Indians or bandits was questioned—but only for a short while.

appointed a U.S. marshal in 1853. On the secession of Texas from the Union, he led a band of volunteers who forced the surrender of federal troops in San Antonio. Then he served as a brigadier general commissioned to raise and command the first Confederate army in the Trans-Mississippi West. In 1862, under General Earl Van Dorn, he commanded the Arkansas, Louisiana, and Texas forces in the battle of Pea Ridge, where he was killed—the day after writing his will.

Like many a Ranger, McCulloch refused to wear a conventional uniform—even as a Confederate. His favorite dress was a plain, dark suit and a brown sombrero, with a revolver as his only weapon.

Advertisement for Colt's pistols of the early 1850's

III. THE TWO FRONTIERS

By the end of the Mexican War, Texas was beyond dispute a state in the union of the United States. Mexico had been crushed, and federal troops soon found themselves in charge of a new and strange western frontier. In the Texas area the land was strange only to the federal troops.

The frontier in 1848 was generally west of a line through modern Laredo, San Antonio, and Fort Worth, but the entire area between the Rio Grande and the Nueces River was dangerous for trader and settler alike. And going west, in 1849 and thereafter to the questionable California gold fields, were groups of prospectors, Texas cattle drives, and a scattering of settlers. They crossed a land largely controlled by the Comanches, Kiowas, and Apaches. Protection was officially in the hands of United States troops: cavalry and infantry. The first federal troops on the frontier, however, were inadequate. These troops, mostly infantry and artillery units, were too few, mostly on foot, and inexperienced. They were not equipped to oppose, much less chase down, well-mounted Indian groups. The day of the United States Cavalry as an effective frontier force was almost thirty years in the future.

Citizens armed themselves to oppose Indian attacks in the manner of ranging companies. Private companies of Rangers were

Peter Hansborough Bell, a Virginian, came to Texas just in time to serve as a private at San Jacinto. He then joined the Rangers and later was appointed inspector general of the republic in 1839.

In 1840 Bell fought at the battle of Plum Creek against Indians and in 1844 was appointed captain of Rangers in the Corpus Christi, or Aransas, district. This area included part of the rough, disputed land between the Rio Grande and the Nueces River. President Houston's brief instructions were to exterminate or expel robbers, murderers, and outlaws. Even at this date, through a direct order from the president of the Republic of Texas, the Rangers were becoming peace officers. And they did not need to bring an outlaw to trial.

When General Taylor arrived in 1845, initiating the Mexican War, Bell and his Rangers volunteered for military duty. Returning from Mexico, Bell was in command of a Ranger force on the Texas frontier, serving almost until his election as governor in 1849.

He was a striking man, tall and slender, with long black hair reaching to his collar and a short growth of beard. As a Ranger, he always wore two pistols and a bowie knife in his belt. In civilian dress he was known for an elegant and modest appearance.

Peter Hansborough Bell

also raised from time to time. One of the last was at Kerrville in 1859.

Small groups of men, able to ride a fast trail, sleep wherever they happened to be at night, live off the land, and strike suddenly and powerfully, were a better answer to Indian troubles than federal soldiers or disorganized settlers. This is precisely what the Texas Rangers were, but financial support and a well-defined chain of command were recurrent problems. After the Mexican War federal commanders in Texas—particularly of the frontier infantry—were given permission to ask the state governor for support companies of mounted men. Still, there was always confusion as to who would pay and what the men were to be called. Often they were called Rangers and supplied their own horses, although the government (federal or state) occasionally did supply weapons. A few Rangers were paid by the United States. Some were entirely in state service. Some were not paid at all.

General G.M. Brooke called on Texas Governor George T. Wood in 1849 for three companies to help guard the frontier. They were to be mustered into federal service for six months. Their efficiency became clear. Before the close of 1851, he had asked for six companies of 79 men each. Some of the first commanders were John S. "Rip" Ford, "Bigfoot" Wallace, J.B. McGown, Henry McCulloch, and R.E. Sutton.

Although some companies of men were mustered into federal service as Rangers in 1854, these years marked the acceptance of Rangers as a special state force, not a type of federal cavalry.

In 1852 Governor Bell called on James S. Gillett to raise three companies of Rangers in Brownsville to deal with troubles in the Lower Rio Grande Valley area. No provision was made for their support. Bell expected them to be taken into federal service; if not, the legislature would provide. Gillett's captains – G.K. Lewis at Brownsville, H. Clay Davis at Rio Grande City, and Owen Shaw at Laredo – raised their companies. The United States secretary of war then replied that Congress had made no provision for the force and the border troubles were only rumors anyway. Some Texans disagreed.

Governor Elisha M. Pease called out six companies of mounted state troops, the first in 1855 under J.H. Callahan. For the most part, these men were intended for border duty. It was a fairly simple arrangement: they were to provide all of their own supplies and await their pay. Such treatment did not seem to discourage recruits, however.

This force on the Rio Grande set a pattern for later Ranger tradition, not only in terms of enlistment, but also for a disregard of the southern border. They soon crossed the Rio Grande into Mexico on an Indian trail, an action the U.S. Cavalry would not take. There they precipitated an international incident by demanding that local authorities turn over renegade Indians to them. They were soon in a fight with a superior force of Mexicans. The Texans briefly captured Piedras Negras, burned many buildings in town, then retreated across the river.

Nor was this the only invasion. Callahan next led a raid into Mexico to recover slaves. The Rangers captured some but were defeated by a Mexican unit, lost several men, and barely made it back to Texas. Callahan was dismissed from the service – but readiness to cross the border became a Ranger tradition.

In 1857 Governor Pease used the Rangers to deal with civil disturbances. He authorized Captain G.H. Nelson to organize an emergency company to prevent settlers in the Karnes County area from attacking Mexican teamsters.

The Rangers were still most often pitted against raiding parties of Indians. In certain cases, Rangers and Indians developed a respect for each other. Blue Eagle, a Comanche operating near the Mexican border, would often trail the Rangers for the sole purpose of watching a good fight – between the Rangers and somebody else.

The same Blue Eagle, long an enemy of Hays's Rangers in earlier years, remarked, as translated by Flacco, that both Rangers and Indians were very brave men, but that he had stopped fighting and thereafter the Rangers would have to go to hell by themselves.

By 1858 Governor Hardin R. Runnels was in office, determined to increase frontier protection. Renegades by Anglo definition, Comanches and Apaches still had the run of much of West Texas. Only a few Indians were on the short-lived "reserves" set up in North-Central Texas. The mounted Indians of the plains were still a formidable threat. Promising opposition, John S. "Rip" Ford

In late 1859 Lawrence Sullivan Ross was appointed as a Ranger captain to lead an expedition against the Comanches. Ross was a short, black-haired, 21-year-old recent college graduate. He was also an accomplished horseman, the son of Shapley Prince Ross, U.S. Indian agent on the Brazos Reserve.

Sul Ross proved equal to the charge. He killed the noted war chief Peta Nacona and recaptured Cynthia Ann Parker in an expedition that helped break Comanche power in Texas. Ross served as a Ranger until 1861, then entered Confederate service, rising to brigadier general. He was one of the most effective cavalry officers in the Southern cause.

He was a member of the Constitutional Convention of 1875, a state senator, then Texas governor in 1887. He "retired" in 1891 to the presidency of Texas A&M College and guided that school as it became a stable and growing institution.

A.J. Sowell at age 23

Our Christmas dinner consisted of parched corn and salt; and to add to our straitened circumstances, it commenced snowing again, and it was almost impossible to hunt.

Without wood; our provisions nearly exhausted; with no hope of getting any, unless we could eat coyotes, we were in a sad fix.

We bid farewell to "Camp Freezeout," as we named this place, without casting one lingering look of regret behind.

—A. J. Sowell

was made senior captain of the Rangers. With government support, he raised another hundred men for an attack on the Comanches in Indian Territory, north of the Red River. Ford's command eventually included some hundred Indians from Texas reserves.

Ford was in a delicate position. He was supposed to cooperate with United States authorities, troops, and Indian agents but to pursue the state's policy of taking Indian warfare to the Indians — even if they withdrew north into federal territory. The Rangers located the Comanches north of the Red River and, in a decisive battle, routed 300. Iron Jacket was killed by a volley of shots as he led his men forward to meet the Rangers. This chief, Po-bish-e-quash-o, always wore a coat of Spanish mail into battle. It made him immune to spears and arrows but not to direct rifle fire.

Indian troubles became fewer, but in 1859 the reserves in Texas were closed. Raids in Central Texas by actual Indians as well as by Anglo outlaws pretending to be Indians had riled local settlers, who also coveted the rich reserve grasslands. Rangers were there to preserve the peace and were often cursed by the settlers when they protected the reserve Indians. The Indians were taken north across Red River into federal territory, and the reserve land reverted to the state.

Ranger units in 1859 and 1860 were the first to include regular Indian scouts. One hundred Indians served with Captain William Marlin in 1858, some thirty rode with "Rip" Ford the next year, and a company of 43 Indians scouted as part of Captain Peter F. Ross' command in 1860. Reports indicated that on occasion these special enlistees did as much fighting as scouting.

To the south the Rangers found themselves on a different frontier. Anglo-American settlement also moved south, and there Rangers were considered the most effective light military force. Where they had often opposed remnants of Indians on the Rio Grande, Rangers now found themselves in conflict with Mexicans. Feelings ran high. The years of the Mexican War had created ill will on both sides of the border.

Juan Nepomuceno Cortina was one of the most controversial figures in the history of the Lower Rio Grande Valley. To many, he was a hero, the first real champion of the rights of Texans of Mexican heritage in that area. To others, he was simply a bandit, a raider, a killer, a troublemaker. Wherever the truth lies, Cortina had a great impact on the history of the Texas Rangers. Reactions to his activities did much to set the role of the Rangers in the Lower Valley for many years to come.

United States troops — some helping with the removal of Indians from the troubled reserves to the north — had vacated Fort Brown when Cortina occupied Brownsville in 1859. After considerable killing and looting, he withdrew, issuing revolutionary proclamations. He sought restoration of the disputed lands between the Nueces and the Rio Grande from which many Mexican owners had been driven after the Mexican War. But, if the area could not be regained, he declared, "our personal enemies shall

Juan Nepomuceno Cortina

not possess our lands until they have fattened it with their own gore." Many Texans of Mexican ancestry rallied to his cause.

With continuing raids Cortina and his men dominated most of the Lower Rio Grande Valley. A company of Rangers was sent from San Antonio under Captain W.G. Tobin but was unable to cope with Cortina. The Rangers were defeated; Cortina's fame grew. He and his supporters had whipped the gringos.

Roma, Texas, c. 1855

"Rip" Ford's Rangers arrived in December of 1859, and the regular army returned to the scene. Cortina began a series of retreats. Between Rio Grande City and Roma, his forces were beaten. He left Texas but was followed into Mexico by Ford and his Rangers. The pursuit was indecisive. After several fruitless raids across the river, Ford withdrew on orders from the new federal commander on the border, Colonel Robert E. Lee.

Cortina may have lost 150 men, the Texans just under a hundred, of whom about eighty were themselves of Mexican ancestry. Parts of the Rio Grande Valley were laid waste by both sides. Such events were enough to cause trouble between Texans of Anglo and Mexican ancestry for the next six decades.

Texas Ranger in the mid-1850's armed with Colt Navy revolver and a double-barreled shotgun

Dr. Rufus Columbus Burleson and Rangers, c. 1875. Most of the names seem to have been lost. Dr. Burleson sits in the center, and two other names are on the image: "Jim" standing at center and Jack Coke standing at right.

IV. CIVIL WAR AND RECONSTRUCTION

By 1860 Sam Houston, as governor, had 517 active Rangers on the frontier and a grand total of about 1,000, counting "Rip" Ford's men to the south. This was one of the largest forces of Rangers ever in the field, on a frontier staffed by about 2,600 federal soldiers. The force was suspiciously large. Some irreverent minds speculated that perhaps the governor contemplated a second war — his own war — with Mexico. But once again a conflict was brewing which would strip regular army and Rangers from the state: the Civil War.

During the Civil War, as during the Mexican War, few Rangers remained in Texas. And few army troops — the Confederacy had other things to think about, and the burden of local protection was left with the state. Various groups were raised for frontier protection, only a few under the name "Rangers," and most were soon withdrawn to enter Confederate service.

The Frontier Regiment was created in 1861 specifically to protect against Indian attacks after the withdrawal of United States troops. The act created a "Regiment of Rangers" and put, at the largest estimate, 1,089 men and 1,347 horses in the field. The force was separate from the State Troops, which was created some months later.

There's a fight on:
everybody get there that can.
— S.P. Elkins

The regiment was "officered according to the rules and regulations of the Confederate States army." Enlistment was for a year; the men supplied their own arms and horses, elected their own captains, and always suffered from a lack of supplies. They were originally intended only for frontier service in Texas, but the state government, under wartime pressures, soon suggested that they be accepted into the regular Confederate army. At first the Frontier Regiment was called "inconsistent with the army regulations" and was not received into Confederate service. By 1863 no one was so fastidious. The outfit was transferred as the 46th Texas Cavalry Regiment.

One regular unit of the Confederate forces bore the unofficial name of "Terry's Texas Rangers" — actually the 8th Texas Cavalry, CSA. Except for individuals, they were in no way Rangers; but the existence of the title does illustrate the power of the phrase.

One Yankee general, a German by the name of Willich, fell into the hands of Terry's men. He inquired who his captors were.

"Terry's Texas Rangers," was the reply.

"Mein Gott," the general said, "I had rather be a private in that regiment than a brigadier general in the federal army." The general may not have been delivering an empty compliment. Willich had lost battles to the "Rangers" twice before.

By 1864 most men were away at war; young boys and old men guarded the frontier against Indians, outlaws, and deserters. These rangers sometimes had to brave prejudice as well as outlaws. It was occasionally said that a man might be in frontier service because he was afraid to be in the regular army. Those who were there at the time knew better.

Very temporary groups, merely called "companies," were raised for the frontier with the added duty of finding deserters or those avoiding conscription. In 1864 "all persons" between 17 and 18 years of age were legally, not actually, enrolled in these frontier companies. Frontier defense had become undependable; at Texas' surrender, civil law was in chaos.

Taylor Thompson and Macedonio Delgado served as Rangers on the frontier in the latter days of the Civil War. Thompson had already served with Confederate forces; Delgado was an excellent tracker, a man of 60 who had lived with the Comanche Indians for 12 years in his youth. These two spent most of their time pursuing Indians west of Uvalde. The frontier was pushed back east many miles during the Civil War in spite of efforts like theirs.

Since my last report we have had hard and bloody work here.

Indians, thought to be Comanches and Kiowas, with some Kickapoo and Lipan allies, had attacked Rangers near Fort Inge, and another two Rangers (one of them the Captain's son) on the Blanco. Another band, perhaps Kickapoo, were located near Uvalde on the Frio. To the south, the Rangers won a bloody battle.

The Indians fought like demons first; and when an Indian tumbled from his horse dead or wounded, his place was instantly filled with warriors from out the second line. . . . Dr. Woodbridge [the Ranger medical officer, who led the group that day], stunned by a blow upon his forehead by an Indian, fell off his horse, but several of my braves, though fighting themselves against overwhelming numbers, came to his rescue, and in a second the Doctor had recovered himself so to join in the work again. His horse was wounded and lost.

I hope that this little lesson given to the savages by that heroic little band of Rangers will do some good; and I am pretty sure that I shall be able to report another success in a few days.

At the same time, referring to my last report, I would like to have some reinforcements; at any rate, to be authorized to fill up my company to the number as organized at first. My men and horses have not had any rest worth speaking of since

For a time after the Civil War, the Rangers were disbanded. Reconstruction laws did not allow groups of armed men to be raised in the South. But the need for frontier protection in Texas did not diminish; indeed, some groups of Indians increased their raids, and banditry was common. Texas became an exception to the general federal restrictions.

In September of 1866 the 11th Texas Legislature called for three battalions of "Texas Rangers"—a rare use of the term. A financing bill followed but failed. Apparently no men were enlisted under the act.

The Constitutional Convention of 1868 asked for establishment of "Texas cavalry volunteers" to guard the frontier. Such protection, under another name, was not long in coming.

The other name was "Texas Rangers." They were raised in 1870 under Radical Republican Governor E. J. Davis. Twenty companies were called for—more than 1,000 men. Citizens of frontier counties were to be recruited for one-year periods. This force, placed under orders of the governor, was funded by $750,000 worth of state bonds, one of the largest expenses of the government. Fourteen companies of the planned total were in the field by the close of 1870.

Like the State Police created to enforce Reconstruction law, the new Texas Rangers occasionally came under fire as the "governor's police." The State Police came to be seen by many pro-Southern citizens not as a peacekeeping group, but as enforcers of an imposed, repressive government. The Rangers were not always exempt from such opinion. In addition, the service was expensive, and the bonds did not sell. The force was reduced to seven companies, and these were often assisted by local citizens in Indian battles. In 1871, for example, many townspeople from Bolivar, including two Black merchants, fought with Company F in an Indian battle in North-Central Texas.

The Rangers of 1870 recovered some 130 head of cattle and 94 horses. They killed 21 Indians and captured an unrecorded number of outlaws. Three Rangers were killed and five wounded. This cost $458,996.15. The record was not spectacular. By June 15, 1871, all had been mustered out of service, primarily because of lack of funds. They were later replaced by a "Minute Man" force, which was possibly even less successful.

Finally, on November 1, 1873, Governor Davis issued an order for seven "ranging companies" to aid the Minute Men. Four were in the field by late 1873, the finish of the Davis administration.

However slight their record, the Texas Rangers of the 1870's did the same job of Indian trailing that the service had done on the frontier for fifty years. All their captains—Richarz, Jones, Kelso, Falcón, García, and Kleid among them—put their names to reports much as Rangers have always done. It was thankless work, forgotten today, and often done without pay.

The State Police was linked to the Texas Rangers in only one way: some men who served in the Police became Rangers. Most famous was L.H. McNelly, one of the first captains of the State Police and later one of the best-known Rangers of all time.

TEXAS RANGERS.
ATTENTION!

DO NOT WAIT TO BE DRAFTED.

The undersigned having been authorized by his Excellency, the Governor, to raise a company of Rangers, under the provisio s of an act entitled "An act to provide for the protection of the frontier of Texas," and appr ved Dec. 21, 1861, has been granted the privilege to receive men from any portion of he State, with a view to select the very best materia the country affords, that efficient service may be rendered.

The act requires each man to furnish his own horse, arms and accoutrements, and I need not say that I wish th m to be of the best kind obtainable---double-barreled shot guns, light rifles and six-shooters, if possible.

The pay offered by the State Government is very liberal and equal to the most favored troops in the service---equal to the pay of any troops of the same class in the Confederate Army.

All persons desirous of availing themselves of this last opportunity of serving their State, are invited to rendezvous at Concrete, De Witt co., on the Guadalupe r ver, on the last day of ebruary, 1862, for the purpose of enrollment and organization the following day, fro n which time they will be provided for by the Government.   **JOHN J. DIX.**

McMullen Co., Feb. 11, 1862.

---

their arrival here. The grass is getting worse every day. . . .

. . . it is not reasonable to be expected that I can always successfully operate in every direction against half a thousand well-armed savages with thirty-eight privates. . . . Though we will not count numbers if we fight, I may lose too many men without having the satisfaction to destroy the enemy. If it were not for this cursed international law, I know very well what to do to clean out these bloody savages on the other side of the Rio Grande.

—Captain H.J. Richarz,
Company E,
in a report of 1870

Rangers at Bosque Bonito in 1890

V. THE FRONTIER BATTALION
AND THE SPECIAL FORCE

The Texas government, under Governor Richard Coke, gave protection to frontier areas with six Ranger companies of 75 men each. These companies, created in 1874, are often called the "first permanent Texas Rangers"; at the time, they were called the "Frontier Battalion." In the next two decades, the new companies—A, B, C, D, E, and F—became typical Texas Ranger units. Later they became legend.

The Ranger camps, sometimes alongside U.S. military posts, marked the frontier, but the frontier was no longer simply a contact line with Indians. The Indians were less of a problem; there were, in reality, few to cope with. The federal Indian Campaign of 1874-1875, carried out by the United States Cavalry partially on Texas' high plains, brought to a close the last significant Indian depredations.

The Frontier Battalion had helped, but other problems remained, problems for Rangers rather than for army cavalry. A class of lawbreakers, murderers, and bandits rose out of the body of settlers, drifters, and speculators in Texas after Reconstruction. Stage and train robbers, feudists, cattle thieves, and fence cutters were on the loose throughout the state. From civil lawbreakers

A short, dapper, well-educated soldier who looked more like a businessman than a gunfighter, John B. Jones commanded the Texas Rangers in a period that saw their rise to fame and their change into lawmen. He had none of the colorful trappings of the movie lawman and remained a cool, calculating field general throughout his career.

Jones was born in South Carolina but grew up in Texas. He was a relatively small man at five feet, eight inches, who weighed about 135 pounds. Like McNelly, Jones was not often recognized—by others—as captain of his men.

Governor Coke selected him to lead the largest segment of the revived Ranger force in 1874, and Jones immediately deployed his men on several fronts—the first, west, to help federal troops put an end to Indian troubles.

Deceptively calm and polite, Major Jones personally rode with his men and shaped the Frontier Battalion into one of the best-known and most-respected groups of Rangers ever in the field.

On many occasions Jones was in the thick of Indian fighting and

in 1874 the Rangers recovered property worth twice that recovered from Indians.

John B. Jones had been named major of the battalion in 1874. He was a quiet, tactful man and a veteran of Terry's Texas Rangers. By 1877 Major Jones had the Rangers reporting on civil crimes, Indian rumors, the weather, and their own morale. Times had changed. In March of 1877 they were ordered to make no more scouts westward in search of Indians unless in hot pursuit.

The adjutant general noted that civil lawlessness was more important than Indian troubles. Rangers, with their great mobility and unquestioned striking power, were everywhere told to assist local authorities in the arrest of known criminals. Major Jones himself defined their new role: "The operations of the companies will be directed, more than has heretofore been the case, to the suppression of lawlessness and crime." Captain D.W. Roberts said, "We hardly knew whether we were Rangers or court officers."

In 1879-1880 the Frontier Battalion rode 1,001 scouts, or actual assignments, and followed 31 "hot pursuit" Indian trails resulting in seven small battles. They also concluded seven outlaw battles of note, killing 12 outlaws, wounding four, and turning over a total of 685 civil lawbreakers to local peace officers. The Rangers, at the request of local authorities, attended 67 court sessions and provided 247 escorts and jail guards. They also recovered some 2,000 head of cattle.

Ranger officers, c. 1880: from left, front row—Capt. Sieker, Maj. John Armstrong, Capt. Bill McDonald; others unidentified.

During the first years of the Frontier Battalion, photography played a role in a Ranger sweep of the Lower Rio Grande Valley. When Company F was stationed at Brownsville, Sergeant Parrott, an amateur photographer, went upriver on a secret mission.

Traveling as a professional photographer by the name of Williams, Parrott was a very popular man. Photographers were something new in the small border towns, and most people wanted their pictures taken—including outlaws. Even the most desperate characters were delighted to pose for the camera. The undercover Ranger was apparently as good a talker as he was

Governor Richard Coke

outlaw cornering. In 1874 some 300 Comanches, Kiowas, and Apaches under Lone Wolf pinned down Jones and a force of Rangers. On this occasion Jones held out more than a day until the arrival of U.S. troops. Four years later Jones personally took charge of the hunt for Sam Bass and was himself on the street in Round Rock when the famous bandit faced Ranger guns.

Jones was appointed adjutant general of Texas in 1879 and continued in this post until his death in 1881.

a photographer. Engaging his subjects in conversations, he found that everyone liked to talk about what he had done. And, in the case of outlaws, Parrott took an extra photograph, which he kept, with a name and information written carefully on the back.

After three months Parrott reported to headquarters, and 15 Rangers moved out, photographs in one hand, pistol in the other.

The sweep was remembered for many years as "the red tide." Some hundred outlaws were "removed from circulation" on the basis of the photographic identification, which, with Parrott's notes, did not allow alibis. Most "trials" lasted no longer than a comparison of the face and the image.

The man Governor Coke sent as Ranger to oppose border troubles in 1874 was a slight man, curly-haired and soft-voiced, who had been a sheepherder before the Civil War.

Leander H. McNelly became the most awesomely ferocious fighter on Texas' southern border. He had served the Confederacy as cavalryman and spy—once successfully disguised as a woman. Though he had been a captain in the hated State Police during Reconstruction, he was thoroughly respected in Texas.

Rangers of Company D, 1878: from left, top row—Doug Coalson, Ed Wallace, Lewis Cook, George Hughes; second row—Nick Brown, Billy Sheffield, R.G. Kimbell, Tom Carson, Dick Russell, L.C. Miller; third row—Ed Sieker, L.P. Sieker, Capt. Roberts, Henry Ashburn, Doc Gourley; fourth row—Tom Sparks, Bob Roberts, Billy Clemens, J.L. Rogers, George R. Bingham, Jim Renick; bottom row—Jim Moore, Sam Henry, E.J. Pound, Henry Thomas.

Brownsville Market House, 1878

When McNelly reached Brownsville almost-open warfare existed along the southern Texas border between bands of cattle thieves and local vigilantes. In addition, Cortina was still active from the south side of the river, and citizens had organized armed groups on the north side. Banditry, both American and Mexican, was an everyday affair. It was a confusing time, but McNelly made his presence known. After one of his first battles near Brownsville, McNelly stacked the bodies of the bandits in the town plaza. He also disarmed and disbanded every vigilante Texan posse he ran into. Occasionally he gave such a group only one minute to put down their arms before he would "consider them outlaws," a consideration few men cared to face.

The Rangers, as usual, developed a potent reputation for both effectiveness and brutality, the choice of term depending on which side of the river or of the law the critic was on. In a short time McNelly was feared and respected by both sides. His men killed many bandits in pitched battles and hanged those they caught. McNelly had his own Ranger executioner, Jesús Sandoval, who frankly took no prisoners. And it was McNelly who, in the Las Cuevas "war," actually invaded Mexico with 30 Rangers. The attack, in pursuit of cattle thieves and a herd of stolen cattle, was initially a failure. The Rangers attacked the wrong ranch, and the assault on Las Cuevas was ineffective.

Leander H. McNelly

John B. Armstrong had been with McNelly at Las Cuevas in 1875. He later served under Hall but was more like his old commander. He opposed bandits and gunmen with a singular passion which helped establish firmly one Ranger tradition started years before: the willingness to pursue a renegade wherever the chase might lead.

It was Armstrong who applied to the adjutant general for permission to work on the capture of the infamous John Wesley Hardin. Hardin, a killer of more than thirty men—and later to become a practicing lawyer and amateur theologian—was a dangerous gunman. Few lawmen could keep up with the tally of his crimes, but he was sought for the death of a Texas deputy sheriff (one of some six recent shootings) when Armstrong took up the trail. A detective went along, but it was Armstrong who directed the chase, which ended in Florida.

When Armstrong found the train carrying Hardin at Pensacola,

McNelly retreated only to the south bank of the Rio Grande and stood off several hundred soldiers and armed civilians. He had a trench dug and prepared to fight the Mexican army with his 30 men. The United States Army was stymied on the north bank, and the State Department of the United States was anticipating a serious international incident. Both were trying desperately to get McNelly out of Mexico. The Rangers had their own international flavor: mixed, as usual. Corporal Rudd, an "Englishman with an education," and a Dutchman, "who had trouble running, but no trouble shooting," were both in the group.

A messenger crossed the river with a telegram stating that the United States secretary of war advised Captain McNelly to return to Texas, adding that United States troops were not to support him while he was in Mexico. McNelly had just finished a pot of slumgullion stew without benefit of silverware when the message arrived.

The captain licked his fingers, wiped the stew out of his whiskers, and read the telegram. Then he chewed on his cigar for a while, sat down on the riverbank sand, and wrote a reply with a pencil stub on the back of the message:

At the Front near las Cuevas, Mexico,
November 20, 1875.

I shall remain in Mexico with my Rangers . . . and will cross back at my own discretion. . . . give my compliments to the secretary of war and tell him and the United States soldiers to go to hell.

        L.H. McNelly, commanding.

Right or wrong, that was the kind of captain he was. He always said he would never send his men anywhere—he would lead them.

McNelly gave the Mexican forces an hour to agree to return the stolen cattle, or he would attack. They capitulated. Later McNelly delivered 75 head of cattle back from Mexico.

His career was cut short by tuberculosis in 1877.

A Ranger group—perhaps in 1874, maybe Company B. Rangers, like close relatives, cast strong images on early photographic plates. Many photographs have been saved for years, long after the original identification was lost. This particular photograph has been claimed as several Ranger groups, including one serving with Jack Hays in the 1840's.

For several years after 1874, the Rangers were actually separated into two groups. The Frontier Battalion, led by Major Jones, was stationed primarily in the west. The Special Force of Rangers under Captain McNelly was at the Mexican border to deal with banditry. McNelly, however, had stopped by DeWitt County on his way south to quell a civil disturbance brought on by a feud — another problem becoming Ranger work.

When McNelly went to the border, Mexican bandits and cattle thieves were the enemy. A few years later outlaws, often very White and very Anglo, were on the scene boasting that the Nueces River was the "dead line for sheriffs." Often, in such situations, Rangers aided local peace officers. The Special Force and the Frontier Battalion now devoted more of their time to thieves and murderers all over the state. The Rangers were becoming peace officers who could trail an outlaw as far as necessary and find him wherever he chose to hide. The Ranger became the gun, a very fast gun, on the side of the law.

The Special Force was reorganized early in 1877 with Lee Hall as first lieutenant and John B. Armstrong, second. Hall had taken command when McNelly's health failed.

That the Rangers remained popular could not be doubted. Special requests for Rangers at court sessions flooded in to the adjutant general of Texas. When the Special Force was considered too expensive to maintain and its cancellation was suggested as an economic move, the West Texas Stock Association offered $7,000 to help keep it in the field.

Some of the most daring Texas Rangers of the late 19th century enjoyed a camp life that included — besides the ever-present duties of caring for horses and cleaning guns — croquet, visits by local girls, and dramatic presentations. Dan W. Roberts wrote of the leisure time for members of Company D when camped near Menard in 1875:

"As time passed on, our neighbors began to think that the Rangers were decent fellows. Some of the Rangers were graduates from the best schools in the country. But their Ranger education was along different lines. They had learned to cope with the 'Wild Bills' and bad men from 'Bitter Creek'. The young ladies and gentlemen began to visit us in camp, and the girls would eat beans with us at the mess table. The Rangers viewed them as beautiful messengers of peace. We could see that social conditions were improving; in a short time you could see some of the 'boys' with standing collars on. Think of it, a Ranger with a standing collar on! They began to name each other 'Society Jake'; '400 Jim'; 'Ward McAllister'; 'Oscar Wilde'; and the like.

"The Rangers made up an amateur troupe and secured some of DeWitt's light draft plays, which they could execute with credit before any kind of audience.

"We had a very good string band. Such were the pleasure hours of Ranger life. They nearly all became good cooks. . . ."

Whatever their dramatic and culinary abilities, Rangers nearly always brought some additional degree of law enforcement to

he stepped aboard to face the outlaw and four of his friends. Armstrong drew his long-barreled Colt .45 Frontier Model, and Hardin said only one thing as he reached for his own gun: "Texas, by God!" A bit later, one of Hardin's companions was dead, Hardin had been knocked unconscious by Armstrong, who wanted him alive, Hardin's three remaining friends were under Armstrong's gun, and Armstrong's hat carried a single bullet hole.

Hardin resolutely claimed he had only killed people who needed killing, but he was soon in a Texas jail.

John Wesley Hardin

Capt. D.W. Roberts's Ranger camp below Ft. McKavett, Menard County, in 1878. The scene, with the grouped men, is at least partially staged.

a frontier town; they more than occasionally became husbands and local sheriffs. Many a Ranger left the frontier service upon his marriage, but Major Jones gave Captain Dan W. Roberts special approval to bring his bride to Ranger camp. Roberts's wife, Luvenia, wrote her own memoirs, which included pictures of Captain Roberts's camp on the San Saba River near Fort McKavett in 1878.

She remarked that riding sidesaddle with a long skirt was difficult, because "it required great care not to expose an ankle, which would have been scandalous."

Mrs. Roberts also noted the spare-time activities: "We were never dull in camp. Several of the Rangers were musical and had their instruments with them. Captain Roberts was a fine violinist. A race track was laid out, and there was horse racing. Card playing was not allowed, and it was not done openly. We had a croquet set, and that game was enjoyed." On one occasion the Rangers

Lamb Sieker, who also served as a Texas Ranger, in the uniform of a colonel of the Texas State Militia, c. 1885

of Captain Roberts's company gave a minstrel performance at Menard as a church benefit.

In these years Rangers were well into police work. Mrs. Roberts remarked that Rangers "were continually making arrests, and invariably they would be 'cussed out' by the wives."

One early morning near Junction, Captain Roberts himself entered a house "without ceremony." A woman confronted him.

"Good morning, Madam," said the captain.

"Good morning, the devil!" began the woman, only the prelude to a thorough Ranger-cursing.

"It was not a pleasant business," recalled the captain's wife.

L.P. Sieker came to Texas after the Civil War and enlisted in the Rangers under the administration of Governor Davis. He later was made a colonel in the service under Governors Ross and Sayers.

When his brother, Thomas Sieker, arrived in Austin to join the Rangers, he was advised not to venture farther west. "The population out that way," he was told, "consists of rough customers." Sieker went on, however, and found a Ranger camp on the San Saba River. The group needed a man, so he was enlisted but told to stay away from Fort McKavett until he had learned the ways of the frontier.

The tenderfoot Ranger soon learned the ways of the West and even recorded a point of frontier etiquette:

"There were bad men in the West in those days. Once I drifted into an eating house at Scabb, a village across the river from Fort McKavett, and found myself in front of eight outlaws seated at two tables. Each one had a Winchester across his legs and a six-shooter by his plate. In such a chance meeting a Ranger always bowed and said, 'Well, boys, too many for me,' and in turn, the outlaws would bow and smile pleasantly, and nothing more would come of it."

Ranger Company C, 1875: from left—John Hart (later sheriff of Karnes County), ? Miller, Buck Harris, and Alfred Allee.

VI. LAW ENFORCEMENT

In changing from a frontier service to a law enforcement role, the Rangers found themselves facing disturbances never imagined in earlier years. One such was the Mason County War, the German-American War, of 1875.

Major John B. Jones received instructions by special courier that help was needed in Mason County. He led the Rangers there himself. On the Llano he was surprised to see 15 heavily armed men rise from behind a stone wall. This was Sheriff Clark with the German faction of a feud originating in cattle rustling that had split the population along ethnic lines.

The Ranger leader found the settlements in a condition much like the penultimate scenes of later Western movies. "I find the houses closed, a deathlike stillness in the place. . . . Every man is armed." One settler was killed while riding down Mason's main street. The assassins then fired into a hotel, narrowly missing women and children, and escaped in the ensuing panic.

The feud had numerous origins, doubtlessly starting in Civil War days when many of the German settlers were pro-Union and many of their neighbors were not. Later grudge killings kept it going until the situation was clearly beyond local control. The sheriff and the justice of the peace were on opposing sides.

Rangers in Cotulla on February 16, 1887

Major Jones and the Rangers helped settle trouble in the area, although accused of partiality by everyone. Through such actions, however, they became known as a peacekeeping force, external enough to any trouble to act impartially, possessed of enough power to contain local men who would break the law by taking it into their own hands, and capable enough to oppose lawbreakers on their own terms.

Writing from temporary headquarters on Silver Creek, Kerr County, in 1875, Major Jones noted some four Indian scouts in a half year, but his words show the Ranger service changing. He wrote that by scouting for Indians on a "different route each time . . . the battalion has rendered much service to the frontier people by breaking up bands of outlaws and desperadoes, who had established themselves in these thinly settled counties, where they could depredate upon the property of good citizens, secure from arrest by the ordinary process of law. . . ." The Rangers arrested and turned "over to the proper civil authorities many cattle and horse thieves, and other fugitives from justice. . . ."

Jones's letter practically becomes a textbook concerning what was happening on the frontier. "The quartermaster found much difficulty at first in procuring supplies for the command at reasonable prices. Parties furnishing supplies to organizations of the kind heretofore having invariably charged exorbitant prices for everything: in some instances, as much as seventy-five cents per pound of coffee. . . ."

After negotiating with a bit of hard cash and many strong words, Jones approved of the quartermaster "having coffee delivered to the companies at twenty-six cents." Besides arrests and supplies, Jones observed the people on the frontier who "seem to think we have rendered valuable service to them, and there is a degree of security felt in the frontier counties that has not been experienced for years before. Many on the extreme border are moving further out, while others from the interior are taking their places, and many more coming with them. The citizens in several unorganized counties think they will have population sufficient for organization very soon. . . ."

Later historians said it no better. At the time, the desperado chose to have no historian, and the Indian had neither alphabet nor ally.

Far to the west, the El Paso Salt War was in the making. This conflict was to be a complicated political situation and civil disturbance that assumed the colors of a race war. It was also an occasion when Rangers both surrendered and lost.

El Paso in 1877 was an isolated settlement, thirty days away from the state capital. Of some 12,000 inhabitants of the area, probably eighty were Anglo-American. Local Mexican Texans had for years freighted salt from the desert east of El Paso. Yet the concept "for years" was in dispute. Many claimed the use of the salt was relatively recent. In any case, the salt was a trade item, shipped into Mexico, and an important money source for a large portion of the population. The salt was free for the taking.

Into this arrangement came Anglos who claimed the land and set up a monopoly on the salt, requiring payment for its use. They also fought among themselves for public and private use of the salt. The outraged former salt gatherers organized both as a political group and an armed force. Soon the arguments grew political, racial—and serious. Charles H. Howard, a Democrat who had control of the salt flats, opposed not only local Republicans, but also the Mexican faction represented by Don Louis Cardis. Howard killed Cardis after a complicated series of incidents created a situation in which Mexican was pitted against Anglo.

Major John B. Jones went to El Paso. He approached the situation typically, saying that he had come to keep the peace, not to settle the salt question. He reminded everyone concerned that he was a peace officer, not a court. After mustering a small group of men as Texas Rangers under John Tays, he quieted the people and returned to Austin.

The Rangers who remained—they were called "state troops" in subsequent reports—started out by supporting Howard in an effort to stop salt wagons. Yet, by the 17th of December 1877, they found themselves surrounded in San Elizario by an armed Mexican force demanding Howard himself. Under siege, with men in his protection, Tays capitulated. Three men, including Howard, were executed by a firing squad. Howard's body was mutilated in front of the assembled crowd while local businesses were plundered. The survivors were released the next day. United States troops arrived shortly from Fort Davis and New Mexico, but the area remained in chaos for some time.

The remainder of Tays's group, led by "the sheriff," in the words of Major Jones, soon were accused of brutal reprisals. Just before Christmas they killed two prisoners who had been in the San

Don Louis Cardis

It is easy to see a graveyard in the muzzle of a Ranger's gun.

—Unnamed outlaw to Ranger W.M. Green (1874)

Socorro, Texas, c. 1850

Elizario mob. Some claimed the prisoners were trying to escape at the time; others who saw the bodies said the deaths were "unjustifiable." Passing through Socorro below El Paso, the group sought out and killed Jesús Telles, a leader of the mob that had mutilated Howard's body.

The group of lawmen also took the time to kill another man, to wound a man and a woman, and to participate in what must have been intended as local terrorism. Official accounts—Major Jones's words—are laconic: "Other excesses and disorders by the state troops and the sheriff's posse are said to have been committed about the same time."

Other Rangers arrived later, and civil peace was restored, but the Salt War was not a glorious incident in anyone's history. During the coming year the Ranger service was both complimented and questioned.

The 1878 report of William Steele, adjutant general of Texas, is typical of many documents reporting Ranger concerns. General Steele solicited county judges, asking about local lawlessness and, not incidentally, the need for state forces in their areas.

Because of a lack of funds, Ranger strength had been reduced to a third of its legislated strength, no more than 25 men per company—and often fewer. The State Militia, sometimes called the "uniformed volunteers" and on duty for short periods, was appropriate for rare insurrection-sized trouble and could garrison only convenient areas. The Rangers remained the most visible, certainly the most mobile, aid to the frontier.

General Steele noted that the "battalion has been spread along from Frio (from where it sent scouts as far as Laredo), along the frontier settlements, to Red River, with a detachment in El Paso county, seven hundred miles from San Antonio." The distance he referred to was not, of course, as the crow flies. "The whole of the vast territory," the adjutant general continued, "is . . . settled in small communities, mostly by stock raisers (cattle and sheep). All of these settlements are subject to raids from the Indian reservations . . . as well as from Mexico and from bands of outlaws who make their living driving stolen stock and taking by force of arms anything that they wish and have the power to take. Stages and small bodies of travelers are robbed by them, as well as by Indians."

Renegades from New Mexico were reported moving into and out of Texas. General Steele had even intercepted letters — some of them love letters — from "desperados." One was a curious mix of invitation to a young lady in Texas and a rather abrupt record of local killings.

"I will write to you again. I am now about five hundred miles from where I written you last. This is headquarters for my gang. I have got ten men with me — the best armed and best mounted outfit you every saw. . . . We just got in off a raid, and made it pay us big. Darling, I am making money fast. . . . If I had you here I would be the happiest man on earth. This is the best country I ever saw, and the healthiest country on earth. We are one hundred miles from the nearest post office. Darling, on the twentieth day of August, Gross and McGuire got into a fight, and McGuire shot him just below the heart, and I shot and killed McGuire. I shot him through the heart. He never spoke after I shot him. We buried him as nice as we could. . . . Darling, I want you to write to me when you get this . . . let me know all the news and how you are getting along, and let me know whether you will come or not. . . . Darling, I have got a Navaho blanket for you that is worth $75; the prettiest thing you ever saw. Baby, take care of yourself, and be sure to write."

The swain may well have been chased out of the state by Rangers, but General Steele does not reveal whether the lady accepted the blanket.

Other letters, from county judges and local sheriffs, attested to the need for state forces in their areas.

Judge A. Blacker in El Paso hurriedly noted that four prisoners in the county jail "could not be held six hours without the rangers."

Thomas M. Paschal, district judge at Castroville, wrote that "numerous bands of bold and desperate men, banded together for the purpose of theft, have been . . . broken up and driven off by the state forces in this district. . . ." The result, he noted, was a "tier of counties now well settled by a large, good class of citizens where four years ago [1874] the war-whoop of the savage almost alone broke the stillness of the prairies. . . ." Judge Paschal heard that the "men who so recently made New Mexico and Arizona a pandemonium were . . . made up of refugees from Texas, driven there by the untiring activity and vigilance of the state forces."

Judge T.M. Paschal

State forces in the late 19th century were not always Rangers; in over half of the cases, they were. In some years Rangers accounted for three-quarters of the theft and murder pursuits handled by the state.

The sheriff of Menard County, J.H. Comstock, said "our county is at present enjoying comparative peace and quiet, but all our citizens attribute it to the assistance rendered civil authorities by the rangers." The sheriff noted that "experience has shown that we have but little to expect from the United States troops, as their movements are too slow and cumbrous. It is well known," he added, "that many bad characters, who are now kept quiet by fear, have often threatened to take revenge upon some of the best citizens of the county for the lawful prosecution and conviction of their guilty friends, as soon as the rangers are taken away."

From the county judge of McCulloch County, B. Campbell, came the opinion that "the rangers are the only officers that have had any success in arresting desperate characters and bringing them to justice. . . . If the protection that is now given to us by the rangers be withdrawn . . . the citizens of the frontier will be forced to abandon their homes to move back into the interior for protection, and the frontier counties of the State, which embrace the finest grazing districts and some of the finest and best farming lands, will be greatly retarded in their development, if not altogether abandoned." And the sheriff of the county, H.T. Eubank, added his opinion, "It is my firm conviction, if it had not been for the frontier battalion, this county would have been overrun with desperadoes and fugitives from justice, to say nothing of the Indians."

A cow hand had to work. All a Ranger had to do was kill somebody or be killed. All they had to do between fights was ride fifty, sixty, or a hundred miles to the next one as fast as horseflesh could take 'em.

—Archie McCoy

A. McAlvaine, sheriff of Tom Green County, entered upon an analysis of why local lawmen and settlers had a hard time against renegades. "To raise a posse and make an arrest is nearly impossible, owing to the sparse settlements and the reluctance which settlers feel towards doing anything to bring upon themselves the enmity of this class of people. Sometimes long distances have to be travelled and the trail followed for days, and . . . citizens dislike the work, and the sheriff who starts on a trip with a posse of citizens is likely to find himself alone at the end of the first day's ride. . . ."

Concerning the last of the Indian threats, the sheriff maintained that the "only possible way to prevent them is to have men who can ride just as far and just as long and a little faster than the raiders. . . . The rangers are the only troops that can do this; and, whenever they start on a fresh trail, they do not stop for a picnic at the first shade." Sheriff McAlvaine considered the Rangers the only defense against widespread outlawry and Indians. He did admit the Rangers could be done away with "if a Chinese wall could be built on the one hundredth meridian, and another on the Rio Grande, to keep thieves and desperadoes out." The State chose the Rangers rather than a second Great Wall. A Ranger company could cover some 12,000 miles of regular patrol in a year.

Farther west, the story was even more concrete, if less flamboyant in imagery. T.A. Wilson, the sheriff of Presidio County, claimed that regular troops were inefficient. Writing from Fort Davis, he said "to the credit of the United States troops," Indians and "marauders from Mexico" had been followed, "but not a single party of them have been overtaken and chastised."

Ranger Company B camped on the San Saba River close to Christmas of 1896: from left—Tom Johnson, cook; Dudley S. Barker; Allen Maddox; John L. Sullivan; and Edgar Neal.

Governor Culberson, from among the rest,

Chose four Rangers, whom he thought best.

He ordered us to San Saba to put down crime—

We met at Goldthwaite, all on time,

Two from the Panhandle, two from the Rio Grande,

Which made a jolly little Ranger band.

We stopped at a hotel to stay all night;

From what the people said, we expected a fight.

They puffed and blowed, and said, we were in danger,

For a bushwhacker didn't like a Ranger.

We laughed at such talk and considered it fun,

But wherever we went, we carried our gun.

—W.J.L. Sullivan
and Allen Maddox

For Indian pursuit, Wilson recommended "a well-organized ranger force, always on the alert, and when Indians commit depredations follow them on cow ponies, leave cooking stoves, wall tents, post traders, iron bedsteads, etc., in camp."

Dissenting opinion there was, but it was minor. Israel Stoddard, county judge of Jack County, inquired closely among the residents of his county and found no necessity for state forces. The rangers and other outside troops formed "no nucleus around which settlements are made," and—although he gave credit to Major Jones for a good job—"the people of the border are better able to protect themselves than they are to raise the necessary revenue to support the frontier forces." A like opinion was noted in the Corpus Christi area.

Yet, to the west—in the words of Judge Blacker of the Twentieth Judicial District—the frontier was a boundary "marked alone by the sword, the pistol, the shot gun, and the rifle."

The consensus was clear. The Rangers were needed.

      ⊛

The Rangers moved with the frontier, or civil disturbances, and by the late 1880's many more were centered farther west than ever before. George W. Baylor had taken over from Tays in El Paso, C.L. Nevill was at Fort Davis, and G.W. Arrington was in the Panhandle.

When Baylor arrived in Ysleta near El Paso in 1879, he encountered some of the last Indian troubles. He participated in attacks on Apaches in Mexico with the Mexican army and with permission of the Mexican government. Later in Texas he followed a band of Indians who had attacked a stage and killed a driver and an itinerant gambler. Some of the Indians – the group itself consisting of twelve men, four women, and four children – had apparently attacked other travelers and herdsmen. Indian attacks were by then so rare that Baylor left on the scout at first simply to determine whether the raids were by Indians or disguised Anglos.

In January 1881 the West Texas ground was frozen so hard that little trail was visible. But closely spaced camps and carcasses of game led into the Sierra Diablo and marked the raiders as Indians. The Rangers were on their last Indian trail on Texas soil.

On the morning of January 29, before sunrise, they came upon the Indian camp. The Rangers and the Indian scouts with them, reverting to a style of attack common years before, dismounted and flanked the camp. As the sun rose they opened fire. All the Indians were killed except one woman and a young girl. Baylor explained that on the bitterly cold morning all the Indians wore blankets, and it was impossible to tell women from men. "In fact," he added, "the law under which the Frontier Battalion was organized don't require it."

Firepower and the license to kill were the chief reputation builders of the Rangers against Indians, bandits, and outlaws; other things are more rarely mentioned. The Rangers themselves had been living on the cold trail, very much like Indians, for days – an outing few local sheriffs would undertake.

As the sun rose higher that January morning, the Rangers burned the camp. They were not after the American and Mexican saddles, the calico, or blankets. There were two pools of near-frozen water nearby. The smaller barely gave them coffee water. The larger had filled with blood.

George Baylor later remembered his thoughts on looking out over their small campfire: "We took breakfast on the ground occupied by the Indians, which all enjoyed, as we had eaten nothing since the day before. Some of the men found horse meat pretty good, whilst others found venison and roast mescal good enough. We had almost a boundless view from our breakfast table. The beauty of the scenery was only marred by man's inhumanity to man, the ghostly forms of the Indians lying around."

C.L. Nevill at Fort Davis and G.W. Arrington in the Panhandle turned to chasing outlaws, even though Nevill continued Indian scouts long after the Indians were gone. Nevill did have the almost unique distinction among Rangers of attacking Indians by boat. Accompanying a surveying party on the Rio Grande, his Rangers took by surprise several groups of Indians, who hardly expected a threat by river. Nevill found boating more dangerous than riding the plains, however; while on the outing, he was almost drowned.

Arrington of the Panhandle had his first military experience in the Civil War. Later he served as a mercenary with Maximilian in Mexico and in Central America. Enlisting as a Ranger, he quickly rose to the rank of captain and was known as one of the strictest disciplinarians among Ranger leaders.

His company found themselves protecting courts and escorting prisoners, patrolling in the middle of feuds, and making minor

George W. Baylor

Bring boys and saddles, hot work.

–Telegram to Rangers, 1890

67

Indian scouts in the Panhandle. On the latter service Arrington at times challenged U.S. Army officers who were, in effect, protecting Indians who were being taken into federal territory.

Most of the Panhandle towns that were founded in the last years of the 19th century had Arrington as a protector. He became known as an iron-willed man whose recurrent and simple report to headquarters read: "I jailed my prisoner."

Sam Bass, coming to Texas for the first time in 1869, drifted into a life of not-very-successful crime, which included only one lucrative train robbery—in Nebraska—but a record of no killings during a heist. The latter helped create a short-lived legend of a beloved bandit.

Bass, and a small group of accomplices, did help establish train robbery as a much-feared activity, although the total haul for Bass in some twenty Texas robberies in as many months was about $500—smaller wages than a cowboy earned at the time.

Yet, somehow, the story emerged that Bass was a bandit king, a Robin Hood character who stole from the rich and gave to the poor. By 1878 Bass had attracted the attention of not only the public, but most Texas lawmen. Adjutant General William Steele and Major John B. Jones of the Rangers had geared up to hunt down the gang. Governor Richard Coke upped the ante by naming Junius "June" Peak to organize a special company of Rangers spe-

Sam Bass at age 16, taken in Indiana before he came to Texas

Sam Bass attempts an escape at Round Rock in July of 1878.

cifically to deal with Bass. Peak had served as Dallas city marshal during the years of Bass' activity and was ready to ride trail.

Rumors were that Bass led a gang of 60 men capable of unified attack and supported by countless spies. As it turned out, Bass could not even organize a successful train robbery, rode with fewer than six companions, including one informer to the Rangers, and was attempting to get to Mexico.

Bass did consider a small bank robbery necessary for traveling expenses and selected Round Rock. On Friday, July 19, 1878, Bass and two companions—a day before they planned to approach the bank—were accosted by a deputy sheriff for wearing guns in the city of Round Rock. Perhaps checking out the streets, the bandits had run afoul of a local ordinance.

Bass, Seaborn Barnes, and Frank Jackson started shooting. Henry Grimes, the deputy, became the first and last person killed by a Bass-organized gang.

Round Rock was, after four on a Friday afternoon, unusually full of lawmen. They had been tipped off to expect the robbery the next day, Saturday. At the sound of gunfire, everyone armed hit the street, Rangers from everywhere as well as Williamson and Travis county lawmen. One Ranger exited the barber shop fully lathered for a shave.

Bass and Frank Jackson made it to their horses and out of town through the web of gunfire, but Bass was fatally wounded.

Ira Aten, c. 1887

Most people would consider the life of the Texas Ranger hard and dangerous, but I never found it so. In the first place, the Ranger was always with a body of well-armed men, which was more than a match for any enemy that might be met. Then there was an element of danger about it that appealed to any red-blooded American. All of western Texas was a real frontier then, and for one who loved nature and God's own creation, it was a paradise on earth. The hills and valleys were teeming with deer and turkeys, thousands of buffalo and antelope were on the plains, and the streams all over Texas were full of fish. Bear caves and bee trees

When he died Bass still had an unsurpassed reputation as a bandit. In death he had the power to inspire both favorable and insulting ballads, but he was no match for the Rangers, even Rangers a bit off guard.

Just before the turn of the century, Rangers were deployed across the state for a wide variety of peacekeeping efforts. For a few years their most frequent use in some areas was against wire cutters.

In 1884 Governor John Ireland called a special session of the legislature. Among other things, fence-cutting was made a felony. The law also said, however, that a gate must be installed in every three miles of fence and that nesters could not be fenced in.

Ira Aten, a sergeant of Ranger Company D, was assigned to the Navarro County area to stop fence-cutting. He and Jim King traveled by wagon to their assignment disguised as farm laborers. Aten soon found out how hard it was to catch anyone in the act of cutting fences, either by watching fence lines after a tip-off or by waiting to be invited along as a potential fence cutter.

He came up with the idea of placing "dinamite booms" on fences, which would explode when the fence was cut. His device was an old shotgun, primed and filled with dynamite and attached to a trip wire. Ranger Aten may have tried it out, because his spelling, in reports to Austin, changed from "dinamite" to "dynamite," showing that he had at least read the box. Although there is no record of a dynamite bomb being used in Texas, the threat seems to have solved the problem.

Aten's letters contain more than new ideas. They show a Ranger trying to come to grips with an unpleasant job in changing times. He was no longer in a position to shoot first and ask questions later: "I want to take the villains without killing them, but . . . I will stand trial for murder before I will stand up and be shot down like a fool." Aten thought little of his assignment: "I will ask it as a special favor of the adjutant general's office never to ask me to work after fence cutters again under any and all circumstances, for it is the most disagreeable work in the world." Yet he was ready to stand by this duty. "You may hear of a killing if everything works right. . . . Nothing will do any good here but a first class killing, and I am the little boy that will give it to them if they don't let the fences alone."

In the course of spying, Jim King and Ira Aten baled cotton, picked 35 acres, and built a rock furnace around a cotton gin boiler, work which Aten grumbled about doing on a Ranger's pay.

Aten had to lie his way into men's confidence, a practice he heartily disliked. When this failed, the dynamite bomb idea was formed. "Should the Governor or the General disapprove of this, all they have got to do is to notify me to that effect etc. They sent me here to stop fence-cutting any way I could and to use my own

abounded. In the springtime one could travel for hundreds of miles on a bed of flowers. Oh, how I wish I had the power to describe the wonderful country as I saw it then! How happy I am now in my old age that I am a native Texan and saw the grand frontier before it was marred by the hand of man.

—J.B. Gillett

Capt. J.B. Gillett on Dusty in 1879

Rangers (and perhaps others) in front of a saloon in Tascosa, Texas, c. 1885

judgment etc. how to do it. And that is what I am doing, and if they will let me alone the balance of this month, I will have my booms set and when the fence is cut, why they will hear of it in Austin."

The governor and adjutant general indeed thought they might "hear of it" in Austin, in the wrong way. Aten was recalled.

Civilization overtook the line of Ranger posts and turned the service into a civil police force. After the last Indian fights in the early 1880's, the Rangers became peace officers whose function was largely to handle trouble beyond the control or the jurisdiction of local authorities. They hunted cattle thieves, opposed mobs, protected court proceedings, and trailed lawbreakers of all sorts beyond the range of the local sheriff or police officer.

As civilization closed in the Rangers were disliked in certain quarters. Some citizens objected to them as merely being a "state police." A few county and city officers resented them because their presence implied that local law could not handle a situation. Outlaws avoided the Rangers because they were, in fact, a potent force. Along the southern border many people of Mexican heritage harbored a thinly hidden hate for the Rangers as defenders of the settlers who had stripped them of land ownership and social position. And the Indians were silent—most were dead or miles away from Texas.

Rangers of Company D of the Frontier Battalion and a U.S. marshal in San Antonio, 1894: from left, standing—
Deputy Marshal F.M. McMahon, William Schmidt, James W. Latham, Joe Sitter, Ed Palmer, and T.T. Cook;
sitting—a man now only identified as a "Mexican prisoner," George Tucker, J.W. Saunders, Sgt. Carl Kirchner,
and Capt. John R. Hughes.

*Rangers from four battalions, headed by Adjutant General W.N. Mabry, assemble to prevent the Fitzsimmons-Maher prizefight
from taking place near Langtry in 1896:* from left, front row—W.N. Mabry, Capt. John R. Hughes, Capt. J.A. Brooks,
W.J. McDonald, Capt. J.H. Rogers; second row—George Horton, J.H. Dvetts, Sgt. Throckmorton, Bob Chew, John Hess,
Creed Taylor; third row—Billy McCauley, Lee Trecn (?), Jim "Wooly" Bell, Ed Flint, James Fulgam (face partially obscured),
Ed Donley, Sgt. S.J.L. Sullivan, Jack Harwell, Bob McClure, Ed Conley; back row—George Tucker, Dr. Lozier,
Ed Bryant, Edgar Neal, Doc Neal, C.L. "Kid" Rogers (on lower step, with cigar), Thalis T. Cook, C.F. Heirs,
John Moore, W.M. Burwell, and Andy Ferguson.

Sam Bates, a member of Company C at Laredo in 1901

VII. THE TURN OF A CENTURY

$\mathbf{A}$t the turn of the century, the charge was raised that under existing legislation only the officers of the Ranger service had the authority to make arrests. It was a serious charge, although only the legal authority was in question, not the facts. The year before, Rangers had made 579 arrests.

Although perhaps based on a technicality, Attorney General T. S. Smith upheld the objection. Overnight, the Frontier Battalion almost ceased to be. Only 24 men served for about a year.

In July of 1901, however, the service was returned to about a fifth of its former strength. The reason was the same: the Rangers were apparently needed. The new law authorized the governor to organize a "Ranger force for the purpose of protecting the frontier against marauding or thieving parties, and for the suppression of lawlessness and crime throughout the state."

Four companies of up to twenty men were authorized. Company A at Alice was under Captain J.A. Brooks; W.J. McDonald started as captain at Amarillo with Company B; Company C was headquartered at Fort Hancock under Captain J.H. Rogers; and Company D was at El Paso with Captain John R. Hughes.

The Ranger captains chose their own men (when not appointed or suggested by the governor), who wore no standard uniform or badge and furnished their own horses—as usual. But now Rangers often traveled by railroad train and were in fact much like a state police force which occasionally used unique methods. It was said that when a Ranger was sent to a frontier town with no jail, he took along a sack of handcuffs. When he arrested a man, he simply handcuffed the offender to a convenient fence or post in the street. Several men so restrained after an evening's patrol was not an unusual sight.

Company F, Frontier Battalion, in 1888: from left, standing—*Frank Carmichael, Bob Bell, "Kid" Rogers, Gene Bell, and Jim Harry;* sitting—*Tupper Harris, Sgt. J.H. Rogers, Capt. J.A. Brooks, Charley Rogers, and Bob Crowder.*

J.H. Rogers—Ranger, Ranger Captain, and United States Marshal

John H. Rogers, a native Texan, was known as a Ranger who always carried his Bible as well as a six-shooter. He entered the service at 19, joining Company F of the Frontier Battalion in 1882, and was made a captain on his 29th birthday. When the Rangers were reorganized in 1901, Rogers became captain of Company C at Fort Hancock. In 1913 he became U.S. marshal for the Western District of Texas, a post he held for eight years. Rogers served intermittently thereafter in the Rangers until his death in 1930.

James Abijah Brooks became a Texas Ranger in 1883 as a member of Captain Josephus Shely's Company F of the Frontier Battalion. He was a 21-year-old Kentuckian and not a tenderfoot. By the time he entered Ranger service, Brooks was already a Laredo cowboy who knew the ways of the border. As a Ranger he played a large part in settling the fence cutters' "war" in Brown County and was promoted to captain in 1887. He served for a while at Cotulla, keeping cattle thieves out of the area, and in 1892 was stationed in Duval County. In 1901 Brooks was made captain of Company A at Alice.

Brooks resigned from the Rangers in 1906. He later became the county judge of Brooks County (named for him in 1911), a post he held until his death in 1944.

Rangers in Alpine, c. 1906: from left, back row—Frank Hamer, Monroe Upton, Marvin E. Bailey, R.M. "Duke" Hudson; front row—Grof White, W.N. Howell, Capt. J.H. Rogers, and John L. Dibbrell.

"No man in the wrong can stand up against a fellow that's in the right and keeps on a-coming." This saying of Captain William Jesse McDonald became what many people have called the Rangers' motto. McDonald lived up to it, bringing to an end enough mob violence and individual troublemakers to create a personal myth and greatly add to the store of Ranger tales.

McDonald was named a captain in the 1901 reorganization. He had already served as a Ranger captain in 1891, as well as a deputy sheriff and U.S. marshal. In 1905 he received publicity acting as bodyguard to visiting President Theodore Roosevelt. A year later he twice walked past military sentries at Fort Brown to personally investigate United States Army troopers after the Brownsville "riot" of 1906. The feat caused Major Penrose to declare that "Bill McDonald would charge hell with a bucket of water," after seeing the two routs of his sentries by McDonald's cool words, "Put up them guns." Major Penrose may not have meant his remark as an unqualified compliment, but it greatly added to the Ranger's reputation.

McDonald survived mobs and more than one ambush, always in the lead of his men. When one Ranger said, "Cap, you're going to get all of us killed, the way you cuss out strikers and mobs," the captain replied, "Don't worry—just remember my motto."

Capt. Bill McDonald

77

Capt. John R. Hughes

John Reynolds Hughes joined the Rangers in 1887 and served continuously until 1915, but it was not his intended Texas occupation. He had lived with the Osage in Indian Territory for five years before deciding on Texas as a location for horse-raising. He moved and set up business near Liberty Hill in Williamson County.

When some of his and his neighbor's horses were stolen, Hughes decided to track down the thieves himself. He became a detective as well as a manhunter. A year later, on a trail that led to New Mexico, he rounded up the outlaws and recovered some of the stolen stock. In doing this he ran afoul of numerous desperadoes, several of whom said they would get him. Ranger Ira Aten met Hughes about this time, and the two became close friends. Aten may have suggested it, but Hughes soon decided that, if he had to be on guard against outlaws, he might as well do it as a Ranger.

Hughes became a captain in 1893, when Captain Frank Jones of Company D was killed. At the height of his activities around El Paso, with several men swearing to kill him, Captain Hughes found the time to serve as a Sunday school superintendent at Ysleta. Yet, for a Ranger, he was unusual in only one way: occasionally he declined to wear a gun.

In the 1901 reorganization Hughes continued as a captain at El Paso. Later he moved to Alice, where his job was the same — opposing cattle thieves and border outlaws — with a new nickname given by both friends and enemies: "border boss."

Hughes died in Austin in 1946.

Ernest St. Leon, allegedly the son of a banished French noble-man and an English lady, was working at the Shafter Mines near Presidio in Trans-Pecos Texas when John R. Hughes arrived to investigate a tough series of robberies. A gang, stealing everything from ore to horses, had proved hard to discover, much less catch.

Hughes made friends with the miner, although St. Leon had been dismissed earlier from Ranger service, accused of stealing provisions. He may have been cleared of the charges but, in any case, was obviously a fine detective who, with the help of his Mexican wife, already had learned all about the stolen ore. Hughes arranged for him to be publicly fired, and St. Leon then went on a staged drunk. He told everyone that he had been fired because of his Mexican wife; furthermore, he was through associating with all gringos and all Rangers. In fact, he would get back at them all, if he could. That very night he was invited to do so.

St. Leon tipped off Hughes, and a few nights later they shot it out with the outlaws. The robberies ended.

Presumably to clear the air, St. Leon left the country for a while but was soon back: John Hughes had sent for him. He returned with a new name, "Diamond Dick," from the gem-encrusted rings he wore. He had perfected his skills as a detective and was a master of disguise, using elaborate makeup. "Diamond Dick's" favorite test for a disguise was to ride up to a Ranger he knew personally and ask if St. Leon was anywhere around just then. If the Ranger sincerely replied no, the disguise was considered a success. He became a useful man. St. Leon's one real fault, only observable when he was drunk, was to try to kill anyone who entered into argument with him. Such an occasion was infrequent. Apparently he either rarely drank, could not shoot straight when drunk, or others rarely picked a fight.

For one season, stripped of his rings and sporting a long, red, theatrical scar down his face, St. Leon went to work as a section hand. He wore a buckskin jacket with long fringe and a Mexican hat with gold stars on the crown. No one seems to have suspected him of being a Ranger at the time, although seventy years in the future he might have been taken as an actor in a grade-B movie. For all his melodramatic show, St. Leon found out who had killed Ranger Captain Frank Jones, then solved a series of other, local crimes. He was also not slow in dealing out his own justice. More than one outlaw fell by the guns of an outlandish stranger.

St. Leon was known as a generous man, once giving Hughes a saddle that the captain had merely admired. He went too far one day, by first arresting, then releasing, three men. The mistake, however, was in standing drinks, several drinks, for the men and himself. "Diamond Dick" was killed in the ensuing brawl.

In the first years of the 20th century, the Rangers preserved their mobility across the state as "ranging" took on yet more new meanings. Captain Brooks and two Rangers escorted eight railroad machinists to Yoakum, where a strike was in progress; at the same time, Captain McDonald brought his company from Amarillo to Cotulla to preserve order during an election, and Captain Rogers protected prisoners from a mob in Hempstead. Often Rangers

An unidentified Ranger, c. 1915

would be called to an area as a nonpartisan peacekeeping force. But, in the minds of some of the public, the new duties were seen as strikebreaking and enforcement of political boss rule.

Rangers occasionally regarded some assignments not to their liking, yet a group sent to Denison in 1922 to police a strike found very different conditions than they had expected. One man remarked, "After months of our own camp cooking, we thoroughly enjoyed the good old-fashioned boardinghouse meals we had during our stay in Denison. We also welcomed the chance to sleep in a bed for a change and dress up in a 'boiled' shirt and neck-tie once more. However, when the strike was over, we were glad to get back to camp again, where we packed our mules, saddled our horses, and headed out across country on a scout."

By the 1920's Ranger scouts in the old sense were rare. The last "chuck wagons" were carried in the back end of a Model T truck, even though the door opened out flat just like the horse-drawn wagon variety. The staples were about the same: flour, beans, coffee, sugar, pepper, salt pork, dried fruit, potatoes, and molasses. But, for the first time, the Rangers also had canned goods, including milk.

The day of the pack mule was not quite over, at least when the roughness of the back country required such transportation. And the only new weapon packed by the Ranger, occasionally, was a Thompson submachine gun.

The Thompson Submachine Gun
The Most Effective Portable Fire Arm In Existence

THE ideal weapon for the protection of large estates, ranches, plantations, etc. A combination machine gun and semi-automatic shoulder rifle in the form of a pistol. A compact, tremendously powerful, yet simply operated machine gun weighing only *seven* pounds and having only *thirty* parts. Full automatic, fired from the hip, 1,500 shots per minute. Semi-automatic, fitted with a stock and fired from the shoulder, 50 shots per minute. Magazines hold 50 and 100 cartridges.

THE Thompson Submachine Gun incorporates the simplicity and infallibility of a hand loaded weapon with the effectiveness of a machine gun. It is simple, safe, sturdy, and sure in action. In addition to its increasingly wide use for protection purposes by banks, industrial plants, railroads, mines, ranches, plantations, etc., it has been adopted by leading Police and Constabulary Forces, throughout the world and is unsurpassed for military purposes.

Information and prices promptly supplied on request

AUTO-ORDNANCE CORPORATION
302 Broadway *Cable address: Autordco* **New York City**

Francisco "Pancho" Villa, c. 1915

VIII. THE RIO GRANDE,
PROHIBITION, AND POLITICS

K ill the gringos!" "Kill the greasers!" . . . familiar words on the South Texas border in the 1910-1920 decade.

Antagonism – and hate – between Anglo-American Texans and Mexicans burgeoned after the turn of the century. Revolutions in Mexico, a world war, then the enforcement of Prohibition and, later, increased settlement in the Lower Rio Grande Valley combined to make the times bloody. The ill-will of past border incidents was only a starting place.

In 1910 Francisco Madero began a rebellion, largely planned in San Antonio, Texas, against Mexican president Porfirio Díaz. Madero, formerly jailed by Díaz, was suddenly in control of some northern Mexican states, and the Rio Grande border became chaotic. The distinction between revolutionaries and bandits was hard for most Anglo eyes to see. And many Mexican citizens fled north, across a border a few of them did not acknowledge, to escape warfare in Mexico.

By 1913, along with the state militia, an enlarged Ranger force was assigned border duty to guard the long river. Many of the tensions there could be directly traced to the actual Anglo takeover only some seventy years earlier. Some Mexicans on the border made it no secret they considered Anglo ownership of Texas, cer-

tainly the area between the Rio Grande and the Nueces, as illegal, brutal, detestable – and reversible. In 1915 a Mexican citizen was arrested in the Lower Valley in possession of a strange document that was to be responsible for hundreds of deaths: "The Plan of San Diego."

This was a revolutionary outline calling for a rebellion of Mexican Americans, Blacks, even Indians and Japanese, in Texas and the American Southwest. All Anglo males over 16 years of age were to be killed. Then, a new republic, open to Black and other minority leadership, would be created as a buffer between the United States and a somewhat-expanded Mexico. Authorship of the document was never determined. Nor was the existence of a coherent revolutionary organization proven. The suggestion was even made that the document was an intentional fraud, written simply to arouse hatred. In any case, Anglos did not take the document as a joke. Hundreds of people were killed in attacks and reprisals on both sides of the border. Rangers attacked to the south, and Mexican soldiers took part in raids north.

More trouble was to follow. During 1916 Pancho Villa, continuing revolutionary unrest in Mexico, raided north into New Mexico. Similar forays followed into Texas, especially in the Big Bend area. Soon more than 100,000 National Guard and regular army troops were on the Texas border – and over 1,000 Rangers.

That Mexican citizens and soldiers killed Anglos on both sides of the border is a matter of record. That Anglos instituted their

If the Rangers were taken away, life and property would not be safe in the Lower Rio Grande Valley.

—A.G. Crawford

84

own reign of terror, with notable Ranger help, is also a fact. The Texas Rangers were involved early and were repeatedly called "the hired guns of the Anglos," among other phrases more direct and obscene. Many Rangers maintained, using their most polite vocabulary, that there was no better friend than the "old-time ranch Mexican" and no worse enemy than the experienced Mexican bandit and smuggler.

Even such polite phrasing did not inspire racial understanding. Yet many Rangers on border duty, as in the 1870's, were Mexican Texans with outstanding records of service. The rolls are laced with their names: Martin Trejo, Juan Gonzalez, Dionicio Acosta, Daniel Hinojosa, Jesús Pérez. It made no difference.

Elizabeth Street in Brownsville, 1914. The view looks southeast from 11th Street.

The Ranger force grew, and, apparently because of political involvement, some recruits were less than estimable. At least since 1911 some Ranger commissions had been offered to pay off political debts. The governor himself had the direct power to hire or fire a Ranger as long as the total number stayed within legislative limits. However, under the pressure of border troubles, the limits rose. Subsequently, "Special Ranger" appointments could be made—400 in 1917 during the war years. These were nonpaid "deputies," who were either delighted to help or who held the appointment simply as a social honor, given as a favor. The category eventually diluted Ranger quality and reputation. It was a period in which certain Rangers did not distinguish themselves.

I have seen the time when the people of Brownsville were afraid to walk on the streets because of the Rangers, and I have seen the time when the people welcomed them to protect their homes.

— Jesse Dennett

William Warren Sterling, adjutant general of Texas and a captain in the Texas Rangers, was the only Ranger to hold all the positions on the force, from private to adjutant general.

Sterling's life was filled with ranching and law enforcement, much of it on the often-troubled southern border of Texas. He was born in Belton but spent much of his life to the south. He enlisted as a Ranger in 1915, served as a U.S. Army scout in 1917, and after the First World War was a cattleman, wildcatter, and justice of the peace.

In 1927 he was appointed captain in the Rangers. He was named adjutant general in 1931 in the decades of political trouble when the lawmen were often split by partisan feeling. Sterling made it clear that he despised the politically appointed Ranger who had none of the true spirit in him.

William Warren Sterling served as a colonel in the United States Army in World War II. He later wrote one of the classic Ranger books —Trails and Trials of a Texas Ranger.

Mexican smugglers with skin bags of tequila, c. 1925

Some of the regular Rangers, too, became politically involved, becoming known as "governor's men," owing allegiance, and their appointment, to a particular governor. When Texas governor James E. Ferguson was impeached in 1917 and replaced by Lieutenant Governor Will Hobby, there "were some changes." The words were not uncommon; often, observers could not tell whether for better or worse.

Ranger troubles on the border centered on the "Mexican bandit," as he was called on the north bank of the Rio Grande. Incidents ranged from illegal entry, through smuggling and cattle stealing, to murder. At times, following tradition, Rangers did not stop a pursuit at the border even in the face of clear orders from both the governor of Texas and United States officials.

The "Goat War" of 1917, a three-hour battle, saw both Texas Rangers and U.S. troops cross into Mexico to find goat thieves. Following a fresh trail and finding branded goats, the Rangers and regular troops fought a pitched battle a mile south of the river at San José. No record tells how many Mexicans were killed—possibly about twenty—but the Rangers were satisfied that the international border would be no protection from pursuit. Mexican authorities were enraged and claimed that a woman had been killed in the assault.

In the Big Bend country, the killing of several Americans during raids on Texas ranches was enough to incite Rangers to attack the Mexican villages of Pilares and El Porvenir. Again they went south, found evidence of robbery, and shot their way out. This incident led to the dismissal of an entire company of Rangers and kept Mexican-Texan relations more than just tense.

Ranger activity elsewhere in Texas during this decade was civil peacekeeping for the most part, but almost all of the shooting and most of the news stories were from the border.

On June 10, 1915, Ranger Jesús Pérez arrested General Benjamin López as he crossed into Texas with the story that he was escaping a revolutionary sentence of execution. The times were indeed most confusing.

As the United States entered World War I, conditions on Texas' southern border did not ease. It was a time of marked anti-German, in fact, anti-foreign, feeling—certainly at the border, where spies and revolutionary agents were especially feared. Mexican Texans always were suspected of being in league with either Mexican national revolutionary leaders or the Germans. They were not the only ones suspect. Everyone with a German name—or any strange accent—could expect to be questioned by Rangers or federal agents. It could be a rough experience.

The international bridge at Brownsville, looking toward Mexico, c. 1920

Ranger troubles came to a head during a legislative investigation in Austin in 1919 which preceded the passing of a new law establishing Ranger strength, duties, and pay. Individual Rangers were charged with murder, torture of prisoners, assault, drunkenness, and being in the pay of German spies. Although the border provided most of the examples, Rangers in Austin were called the "poker-playing club" on the floor of the Texas House of Representatives. It was suggested that the only qualifications Rangers had to have were reputations for killing and insolvency. A legislator did point out that "they usually had both."

State Representative J.T. Canales of Brownsville opened the formal investigation into Ranger activity. The testimony included evidence of many illegal and brutal actions on the part of individual Rangers, while it indicated, clearly in the consensus of the legislature, the need for such a service.

The Rio Grande at Brownsville, 1916

Of no particular support to Ranger defense were four men, including two regular captains and a Special Ranger, who picked the time of the legislative investigation to go out drinking – and shooting – near Austin. One of the Rangers was shot and killed by another during a coin-flipping game. It was very hard for the adjutant general's office to claim that there were no excesses in the service.

Some measures had to be taken, some restraints imposed. The committee report declared that the Ranger force was badly needed along the border of Texas, but it condemned the acts of murder, execution, and other "arbitrary and overbearing" acts of certain Rangers that committee members considered proven. The service was cut from about 1,000 men to 76, and clear limits were placed on their activities. Allowed equipment was not lavish. The legislation required that "members of the force" equip themselves, but allowed the State to pay for a horse – *if* it was "killed in action."

The southern border itself seemed strange to many people in Texas. The question of removing the Ranger service was a topic lending itself to satire. In March of 1919 the *Dallas Morning News* noted that "Thomas B. King took the position that the State should get away from the border and permit the Federal authorities control along the Rio Grande. He pictured," the newspaper claimed, "a military highway along the river, with shade trees on either side, and recommended huts along the route, with both American and Mexican women serving the citizens of both countries."

Whatever humor or typographical error may have crept into the 1919 investigation, Ranger conduct and activities away from

There is more danger from the Rangers than from the men they are supposed to hunt down. . . . they are the most irresponsible officers in the state.

– Representative Cox

the southern border were hardly mentioned. These were considered to be a minority of cases, and, where there were reported Ranger "excesses," civil suits were already under way.

But, whatever the criticisms, in the West the Texas Rangers were models for other state or territorial peace officers. Arizona, Oregon, New Mexico, Nevada, Colorado, and California tried central police or ranger organizations. Three Texans, at least, served with the New Mexico Mounted Police: George Elkins, Charles R. Huber, and Rafael Gomez. In later years a few Texas Rangers drifted west into the service of the Arizona rangers.

And in Texas the service was seriously questioned, criticized, and condemned. Yet the need for Rangers always drifted to the top of the arguments—and stayed there. The legislature, at least, had answers. Did the Rangers perform a needed service? Yes. Was Texas ready to do without them? No.

A staged photograph of a Texas Ranger removing whiskey from Mexican bootleggers at Brownsville, c. 1920

National prohibition of alcoholic beverages lasted from January 17, 1920 (and in Texas from May of 1919), to one minute after midnight, September 15, 1933. Along the Texas border liquor smuggling became rampant, and Rangers were assigned the additional duty of helping federal border officers in such matters. Within the state Rangers were given the task of finding and destroying illegal stills and the resulting bootleg whiskey. A few Rangers quit the service.

The southern border of Texas, 1,248 miles of river, afforded many places of opportunity for smugglers. Rangers were ideal officers for patrolling the less-populated stretches. They went on scouts as long as sixty days, camping all the way.

No body of men has been more acclaimed for valor and efficiency than the famous Texas Rangers.

— Maude T. Gilliland

89

As it always had, in the earlier 20th century, the service attracted men who were individualists and who often added to the larger-than-life image the Rangers projected.

One of the best-known Rangers was M.T. Gonzaullas, often called the "last of the two-gun Rangers." By any definition, he was not the last, but he is credited with killing 22 men in the line of duty. The total he admitted to was "several."

Gonzaullas was born in Spain, the son of a Portuguese father and a German mother. The family traveled a great deal and was in Galveston in time for the hurricane of 1900 which destroyed the city and left Gonzaullas a nine-year-old orphan. Little is known of his early life, although claims are made for his being a mercenary in the armies

"Regular" Ranger stations were at rented houses near the larger cities: Laredo, Hebbronville, Brownsville, and Rio Grande City. These houses usually had lights and water and a wood or gas stove, but no beds. The Rangers would simply put their bedrolls on the floor.

Ranger salaries in the 1930's were $90 a month, plus $30 subsistence. Automobiles were more essential than horses by 1930; the Rangers supplied their own, even though the only travel allowance some years was a railroad pass. But the idea of a man providing his own equipment (including the rifle and pistol out of his first paycheck) had become more than quaint. The Rangers were often in sore need of equipment and operating funds.

In the 1920's and 1930's, the Rangers had more to do than chase smugglers and cattle thieves on the Rio Grande border. Again they became a statewide force, keeping the peace in touchy situations. Labor troubles in Galveston in 1920 brought Rangers into the port city, where the State had taken over the police administration. Rangers were accused of protecting company interests and were assigned duties that went from guard work during strikes to ticketing speeders. In less than four months, the Rangers at Galveston made 1,510 arrests.

This level of activity, little of it heroic stuff, was not uncommon. Texas Rangers were used against lawbreakers of all types in labor disputes, gambling houses, bootlegging, and general crime from murder to vagrancy. There were occasional moments of other activity: in 1924 Rangers on a leave of absence were judges at an international riding exposition in London.

The Texas Ranger service, from the turn of the century until 1935, often was linked directly to political interests — very questionable political interests. Years before, a critic had remarked that Texas would go to hell under Ranger rule. Major Jones responded that, if Texas did, it would go according to law. In the 1930's even that assurance seemed weak.

Any governor could name the state's adjutant general, head of the Rangers, and could also appoint, or influence the appointment of, any Ranger. James E. Ferguson, William P. Hobby, and Miriam Ferguson were among those fondest of appointing "their own" men to Ranger service. One of the most spectacular changes of command came after the election of Mrs. Ferguson to her second term in 1933. Adjutant General Sterling quit his office — and forty Rangers left with him.

Ranger identification of Manuel T. Gonzaullas

Governor "Ma" Ferguson, along with the legislature, cut Ranger salaries and the service itself to 32 people. Transportation money was so reduced that Rangers often had the choice of paying their own way or remaining at headquarters. Then Ferguson simply discharged the force and recreated it with her own appointments. As it turned out, many of these men were later accused of various crimes including extortion, gambling, bootlegging, and theft. Her appointments of Special Rangers reached the ridiculous total of 2,344 (including some ex-convicts). Many were simply honorary; some brought shame to the service. A popular comment was that a Special Ranger commission could be had with more ease, and with less good reason, than a Kentucky colonelcy. Ranger commissions became a farce.

By 1934 Rangers from South Texas had allegedly confiscated gambling equipment and opened their own establishment in another town. One Ranger captain was charged with owning several gambling houses and saloons, raiding rival enterprises for the needed equipment.

of both Mexico and China and serving as a Treasury Department spy. One of his several Ranger enlistments was in Jerry Gray's Company at El Paso in 1920.

During Prohibition Gonzaullas served as a federal agent, then reentered Ranger service as a sergeant in 1932. In that year a "wealthy oil man" bought a car for him which was to become famous: an armor-plated Chrysler fitted not only with a "Texas Rangers" sign below the license plate, but also bullet-proof glass and a submachine-gun mount.

No less famous a man was Frank A. Hamer, who is well known for participating in the ambush of Bonnie Parker and Clyde Barrow. Hamer was not in Ranger service at the time but had a long record of duty as a Ranger, marshal, and private detective. He amassed formidable statistics. He participated in at least 49 gunfights, including several in which he was left for dead, killing some 52 men in his lifetime — and one woman, Bonnie Parker. At his peaceful death in 1955, Hamer was said to carry some 23 gunshot wounds and about 16 bullets and lead fragments in his body.

Governor James V. Allred and Texas Rangers, c. 1935

One rather notable Special Ranger appointment by Governor James V. Allred in 1938 was Mrs. Frances Haskell Edmundson of San Antonio, chairperson of the Womens' State Democratic Committee and a deputy sheriff of Bexar County. She was named a ranger to organize Texas women in a drive against the use of marijuana.

Instability of this kind could only wreck a law enforcement agency. Time for reform had come again.

When James V. Allred became governor in 1935, one of his first acts was to cancel all Special Ranger commissions and do some selective firing among the regulars. In August 1935 the Texas Rangers, then 34 strong, were placed under the Department of Public Safety, a new state agency which also received the Highway Motor Patrol, formerly under the Highway Department. In addition, this legislation created an identification bureau, a scientific crime investigation laboratory, and other support units needed in a complete state police system. It was not long before Rangers were using very modern law enforcement methods.

The number of Special Rangers was limited to 300. Their powers were restricted to enforcing laws protecting life and property when the regular Rangers needed help. They were intended to be real deputies, and, although some appointments continued to be criticized, a commission was harder to get.

Regular Rangers were to be chosen by the director of the Department of Public Safety with the approval of the new three-member Public Safety Commission. The governor could only recommend appointments, no longer hire and fire at will. Rangers were also, for the first time, restricted to territories. The state was divided into five districts with a captain at each headquarters under the central division. Ranger privates received duty stations scattered in each district and could leave their territories only by direct order, though they still had statewide jurisdiction.

At first, Rangers did not have state-owned patrol cars but received car allowances. They did receive state-owned horse trailers, however. Equipment for the Ranger service greatly improved.

In 1941 there were four companies of Rangers in addition to the headquarters unit. The staff totaled 25 Rangers and five criminal investigators.

IX. MYTH AND TALL TALES

Ships, baseball teams, automobiles, books, airplanes, condoms, newspapers, dramatic presentations, motion pictures, musicals, and a hundred other things, some best forgotten, have used the name "Texas Ranger."

The Ranger himself has given rise to some of the most outlandish fiction ever written and some of the wildest brags to come out of Texas. The Rangers have been called the most celebrated Texans in America, mentioned in poetry from Walt Whitman to the present day, glorified and damned in some of the most unbelievable anecdotes of the West, and put on the clichéd stage and screen as heroes or devils, with but one common element — the superlative.

From the early 1930's the cry of "Hi-Yo, Silver, Away!" has been well known — in fact, known to a listening, viewing, and reading audience estimated at 90,000,000 a week in 1955. Radio, television, books, newspapers, and comic books brought the Lone Ranger into most homes, when people weren't at the movies, to become one of the most popular fictional heroes of all times — ranked with Robin Hood, King Arthur, and Zorro. And about 55 percent of the audience was adult.

The Lone Ranger was directly inspired by the Texas Rangers. George W. Trendle created him in about 1932. A fellow writer working on the character as a commercial project saw him as a happy-go-lucky cowboy who shot down various outlaws while laughing. But Trendle thought of him as an example of good living and clean speech. He decided on a thoroughly Western character, a man of action, a hero completely on the side of right and justice. Almost immediately Trendle decided "he could even be a former Texas Ranger."

And the Lone Ranger was born.

John R. Hughes tries out a modern motorcycle, April 19, 1940. The former Ranger captain was on a visit to the Texas Department of Public Safety.

John R. Hughes is thought by some to be the original of the fictional Lone Ranger, but it is unlikely that he was the only model, although Zane Grey almost certainly used Hughes for *The Lone Star Ranger*.

In any case, the fictional history of the Lone Ranger began when six Texas Rangers were ambushed by an outlaw gang. All apparently were killed, but during the night an Indian chanced by and discovered one Ranger still alive, though gravely wounded. The Indian, Tonto, had been a childhood playmate of the Ranger and now nursed him back to health. The Ranger, later marking six graves at the ambush site—one empty—assumed a mask to keep his identity secret while on the trail of the outlaws. This taken care of, the Lone Ranger went on to right many wrongs in thousands of following episodes.

Much of the wind of time blows between the ranger of 1823 Texas and the fictional Lone Ranger. Price Daniel, a senator in 1955, speaking from the *Congressional Record*, claimed the Lone Ranger "program has served as a vital factor in keeping alive in the minds of people, both in the United States and abroad, the traditions and ideals of the Texas Ranger organization and its work in maintaining law and order." It had already worked the other way around. Twenty-three years earlier, the reputation of the Texas Rangers helped create the masked man. And certain stories are still told.

The Texas Ranger arrived by train in the oil boom town, called for when mob violence passed beyond the control of a local sheriff. The sheriff, meeting the train himself, shook the Ranger's hand, then looked around with a worried expression.

"Where are the other Rangers?"

The Ranger took only a moment to reply, looking past the worried sheriff with a glint of steel in his eyes and letting his hand fall gently on his pistol.

"You've only got one mob, haven't you?"

This particular Ranger has been riding by horse or railroad into an oil town, range war, or feud in practically every story written about the Rangers. He is always alone. He always has piercing eyes. He always talks the same.

The incident probably never happened exactly like that. It cannot be traced, except to a similar story told about Captain Bill McDonald, but his is only one among many stories of a Ranger quelling an entire mob, outdrawing a gunman, turning the tables on a particularly troublesome group of lawbreakers, or simply walking up and disarming a man who had barricaded himself and held off other officers for hours—perhaps days. The only truth to these stories is that they have happened. Not often, but frequently enough to become retold stories and Ranger tradition.

So, the story of the Ranger who alone deals with a mob, or a single gunman, is enduring myth—and occasional truth.

"From what I've been hearin' jest one of these here Ranger fellows can take on a whole Comanche tribe, if they're a-mind to, or a whole endurin' rustler outfit of them sidewinders that hole up in this Llano country, and clean 'em plumb out without even half tryin'."

"Mebbe. I'm sho a-hopin' so. This here country needs a good cleanin' and if ever they was a job for the Rangers it's this here we're a-lookin' at right now. . . ."

—J.E. Grinstead,
Texas Ranger Justice

Desdemona, Texas, an oil boom town known as "Hogtown," c. 1920

The Rangers even inspired folk songs, which traveled from the New World to the Old—not the usual direction. In Aberdeen, Scotland, a version of "The Texas Rangers" begins:

I saw the Indians comin',
I knew their savage yell;

My patience at that moment
no mortyal tongue could tell;

I saw their glitterin' lances,
their bullets round me fell;

My mind wis bawnt on ranging,
a-rovin' fore-'e-well.

And ends:

Come a' ye's gallant rangers
aroun' me here this night

Whativir you do for a livin',
for God's sake nivir fight,

Your enemy is quite careless,
they shoot right in the crew—

They're boun' tae hit somebody
an' perhaps it might be you.

Even if the last quatrain is not entirely in the most robust Scottish tradition, there were many Scots who became Texas Rangers. A few may have returned home. Yet, today in Scotland, no one seems to know just how the song arrived there.

Taken at the Menard Texas Rangers' Reunion, 1922 (?)

M.T. Gonzaullas, October 16, 1951

X. A SOMEWHAT DIFFERENT IMAGE

Over the past few decades, the Texas Rangers – the service and the men themselves – have changed. They still have that brand of personal bravery and sense of duty which is tradition. They still do not hesitate to use sheer firepower if the occasion demands. They still are defenders of the law, through and through. But they no longer distribute frontier justice as fast as a revolver can be fired; few Rangers ever did. They no longer seem independent of higher authority; earlier Rangers often did. The Texas Ranger service is assuming a somewhat different image. For better or for worse, they are no longer the "gunsmoke and saddle leather" bunch of a century ago. Neither are they faced with the very real possibility of not surviving a legislative session, as was the case a few times in the past.

Far from becoming superfluous highway patrolmen, as some thought a generation ago, they are still a significant part of the Texas Department of Public Safety: lawmen who can, upon request, help anywhere in the state in cases of major crime including murder, riots and insurrections, fraud and theft, fugitive search and apprehension, and government corruption. The Rangers are trained by the DPS, the FBI, and other agencies in modern investigative skills. And they no longer must own a horse or even know how to ride one.

One captain is quick to point out that Rangers in the southern and western parts of Texas do occasionally need a horse. There are still cases of cattle theft and fugitive search in desolate areas. Some Rangers now borrow a horse when necessary.

More than one rural Ranger calls his urban counterpart a "concrete" Ranger. The term is affectionate. It says nothing about a Ranger's integrity or bravery or ability to enforce the law. These things are taken as absolute, inflexible standards. The word merely means that a Texas Ranger in Houston obviously spends a lot of time on concrete. Of course, one can also hear that a Ranger

Rangers looking for clues at a burglary scene

is not a "real" Ranger unless he's in the mesquite. One doesn't hear this too often. And only in the west.

Some Rangers—those in the cities, of course—do dress a little fancier than others to the west. But the differences are minimal. There's still no uniform. A decade or so ago, unofficially, there was a uniform: the tan gabardine suit. No longer—the only official item of dress for a Ranger, and it can be individual in detail, is the circular Lone Star badge. But much is set by custom. All Rangers usually wear Western hats and boots. All wear suits in town or for official gatherings. And all wear ties except when in the field. Other DPS employees shed ties, with bureaucratic approval, in the summer—not the Rangers.

And they all, at last sight, shave.

And the eyes: not all Rangers have piercing, gunmetal eyes, but there's always something there. The typical Ranger seems to look carefully into far distances whether that be toward a horizon or into someone's face: more than just alert—a sharp confidence not seen often today.

Rangers "somewhere in South Texas," 1933

Rangers still have the reputation of being awesomely armed. They have posed for photographs with everything from bazookas borrowed from the army to personal sidearms with bores like water pipes. What they are issued is a revolver, a 12-gauge automatic or pump shotgun, and a Ruger Mini-14 semiautomatic rifle. Anything else they wish to carry, as a personal sidearm, they may—provided it is at least as large as a .38 and they qualify every six months in its use.

Ranger George Burnup and Lester Robertson of the Texas Department of Public Safety on an armored personnel carrier, September 19, 1955

*Company E at Midland,
November 20, 1970*

When necessary, they are issued bulletproof vests, tear gas guns, grenades, infrared night scopes, and, in short, any equipment a lawman might need. But their armament is still only a detail of the service, although one that holds public interest.

What are not details are the things making the service unique today. First on the list is reputation. Some would call this the "myth" or "esprit de corps," while others would say "lies" or "the record." Often it's called an individual sense of duty and bravery.

Whatever it is called, it's real. Both inside and outside the service, the Ranger has a reputation. He is a reputation. Rangers in the service describe this as something one must live up to, something forged by earlier men in the service but present in every Ranger today. Some call it integrity, or duty, or an ability to get the job done. In earlier times it might have been the real ability to outgun three men on a dusty street. Today it can be jumping between a victim and a knife-wielding assailant with no hesitation; moving a child out of the way before returning pistol fire; or digging, once again, again for the fiftieth time, for evidence of voter fraud long after everyone else has given up.

Rangers are, of course, involved with things other than crime, tradition, and controversy. They ride in parades, take part in civic activities, and lead fairly usual private lives, even though they are on duty 24 hours a day.

Rangers have acted as advisors for movies and dramatic productions. More than one has been involved with show business in some form. Ranger Joaquin Jackson, after arresting Johnny Rodriguez (more or less for goat stealing), arranged for the young man to audition as a musician. Rodriguez became one of the first Mexican-Texan country-western singers after his brush with the Rangers, and Jackson, after his recent advice to moviemakers, became "Hollywood" Jackson – to a few friends within the service, that is. *Extreme Prejudice* was a typical recent Ranger movie – at least featuring a Ranger as a main character dealing with crime almost as powerfully bizarre as that which opposes Agent 007, James Bond. The movie needs no careful review. The Ranger – moving coolly through hails of bullets, showdowns on the street, complicated passions, a turgid plot, and the heat of the Texas border – wins. And the Ranger wins, in part, by taking the law into his own hands.

Today, by law, the Ranger service has statewide jurisdiction to investigate any major felony. Rangers apprehend criminals; deal with riots; investigate instances of local government corruption; work major cases of theft, murder, or rape; and deal with criminal cases crossing lines of local jurisdiction. Almost all of this is by invitation from local law agencies. Rangers can be assigned to any case by order of the state government or by a grand jury,

even in instances where local law enforcement agencies have not asked. But the latter, usually, makes for bad relations.

It has happened. And, when it does, one captain deals with the situation by sending in a Ranger from a location in the state different from that of the job. Most of the time Rangers are invited to help with a case, and often they are invited by police departments in smaller towns or by sheriffs in rural areas.

Obviously Rangers can help in an investigation where information is required from an area distant to a police department which does not have personnel or funds for travel. Since the Rangers are a statewide service, a man stationed near the source of possible information is assigned as part of his regular duties. Across Texas is a long way. If Beaumont lawmen need information from near Dalhart in a hurry, a Ranger is a logical person to ask.

And, equally obviously, if a sheriff seems to have discovered voter fraud or mishandling of county funds by local officials, it might be a whole lot easier, certainly more prudent, to call the Rangers. In fact, investigation of local government has become a widespread Ranger activity not often noticed by the public—except where it happens.

There are cases where a Ranger was sent in to look at one suspicious activity, did that successfully, and was asked to stay on to look at another local, but unrelated, activity. Recently in South Texas a Ranger was sent into a county to investigate what appeared to be an illegal speed trap run by a judge and a commissioner. The initial investigation led to a conviction, but no sooner was this settled than the Ranger was officially asked to remain to investigate an administrative aide in city government. The main clue handed to the Ranger was the simple statement, "We think there's something wrong." There was—about $10,000 in stolen money. When this investigation was completed, the Ranger was told that there just might be something amiss in the water district—again, something about public funds being mishandled. At about the same time, the Ranger office received a call claiming that someone in the local district attorney's office was illegally taking money, but it sure would be hard to prove. . . .

The Ranger may still be there. At last count, requests for investigative aid had come in concerning other branches of the county and city government, a parks system, a purchasing office, and the local trash department. The reputation of the Ranger service has always been that "they get the man they are after." Rangers are now creating the tradition that they can get the facts. Evidence which will convince a local grand jury can be hard to come by.

And investigation of voter fraud is an activity increasingly involving Rangers. Several individuals have attained the reputation of knowing more about determining fraud in voting procedure "than 99 percent of the lawyers in the state."

Cynics have mentioned that Texas is a prime place for chasing fraud or government corruption because there's so much of it. Such a statement smells of opinion, but Rangers do have a good record of providing evidence leading to convictions. In fact, in monetary terms, the Rangers seem to be an efficient operation.

Funding is just over $3.5 million a year, about 80 percent for salaries. Recent levels of work in a year have included more than 5,000 investigations, some 1,300 felony arrests, and more than $9 million in seized contraband and recovered stolen property.

Texas Ranger Ron Stewart (right) works with local officers to recover stolen dinosaur tracks. This case involved the theft of dinosaur tracks, millions of years old, preserved in Texas limestone. In the modern world, as in the old, crime takes many forms.

State funding through the Department of Public Safety in recent years paid for a service of 96 Rangers and 15 support personnel in the state. The six companies are still called A, B, C, D, E, and F with a "headquarters company" in Austin consisting of one man, who works that city and all state property—which is a lot—around town; state hospitals and schools are included.

The service is under the command of the senior Ranger captain, in turn under the supervision of the chief of Criminal Law Enforcement and the director of the Texas Department of Public Safety.

They are not the only "rangers" around these days, but they are the only official ones. Today the so-called "Special Rangers" are a diminishing category. Formerly somewhat of an honorary designation, the title has changed. The Cattle Raisers Association of Southwest Texas, as well as some railroads operating in the state, do employ private officers with what are called special ranger commissions as bonded guards, but they are not connected to the Texas Rangers. Many organizations, such as "neighborhood"

Lee Roy Young Jr.,
Texas Rangers, Garland

rangers, use the name in a generic sense. And a Department of Public Safety employee with more than twenty years of service can apply for a special ranger commission. Such peace-officer retirees may still carry their guns and work privately but are not counted as in the Ranger service.

The makeup of the modern Ranger service, in terms of ethnic groups, is still predominately Anglo. In recent years Hispanic Rangers have numbered under 10 percent of those employed by the service. In September of 1988 Lee Roy Young Jr. became the first Black appointed to the regular service. Young was a Department of Public Safety veteran working in criminal intelligence. Like many Rangers, Young sees his appointment as the fulfillment of a long-held dream – and simply a slight shift in Ranger image. "I'm just going to be the newest change."

The men themselves no longer come directly from sheriff's or police departments across the state, although they may have had such employment. A change in requirements demands that an incoming Ranger have a total of at least eight years of commissioned law enforcement service, the last two years of which must be with the DPS. Some qualified persons may be missed with such a rule, but the service knows the men it inducts – knows them very well indeed. And, because of this, exact "Ranger requirements" no longer exist. DPS requirements include college training and experience with military or civil police. Ranger appointments are made on the results of a competitive examination and oral interviews, which some applicants have failed several times. The number of applications for an open Ranger slot has varied from about 200 to ten. In recent years some thirty to forty applicants have been on hand for each opening.

Rangers often are seen not as individuals, however, but as a group in the light and opinion of the observer. To some people, Rangers are a necessary peacekeeping service which is efficient and fair precisely because it is not connected with local police and sheriff's departments. Others claim that the Ranger service is a thing of the past – or should be: an unnecessary, old-fashioned battalion comprising men who delight in posing as government goons to restrict civil rights and who glory in brutality.

Ranger reputations tend to polarize observers. The stories are so powerful that even newcomers to Texas soon hear of the Rangers and quickly have an opinion. Rangers are particularly disliked by many Texans of Mexican descent. The years of border troubles followed by decades of labor disputes left many scars, in spite of the scores of Texans of Mexican heritage who have served, honorably and for long periods, as Texas Rangers.

Typical criticism centers around the former presence of Rangers in political and labor disputes – almost always in South Texas. In Crystal City in 1963, political candidates for the city council were racially polarized when the Rangers were sent to keep the peace during local elections which appeared to be headed for violence. The election of Los Cinco Candidatos to the council was allegedly opposed by Rangers who were said to have harassed both candidates and voters. The most controversial figure was

"One Riot, No Rangers –
One Strike, Many Rangers"

–picket sign at Laredo, 1967

Texas Rangers at the Capitol in Austin, ready for a possible riot, May 6, 1970

Ranger Captain A.Y. Allee, who attended city council meetings and roughed up the mayor—for good reasons or bad ones, depending on the side of the observer. But verbal attacks on the Rangers avoided a position of "it-depends-which-side-you-are-on" rhetoric. The arguments were in absolute terms, and, whether right or wrong, the Rangers were accused of being too violent, acting as an obstruction to legitimate protest, and being unnecessary to keep the peace.

Likewise, Rangers were said to be acting as simple strike-breakers in 1966 and 1967 in Starr County. Newly formed unions did not appreciate having their lines crossed or their right to assemble threatened—whether in the name of the law or not.

A Mexican-American Joint Conference was held in Laredo in May of 1967 headed by Dr. George T. Sanchez. This citizens' investigative group passed resolutions soon made very public. Members of the group, considering evidence in their hands concerning the way the Ranger service had been used by the state and how individual Rangers had acted, called for the service to be disbanded. The Texas Advisory Committee to the United States Commission on Civil Rights thereafter held a closed session. Their deliberations ended with the statement that "denials" of legal rights in Starr County included "physical and mental abuse by Texas Rangers and Starr County law enforcement officials." Senator Joe Bernal was a bit more direct. As quoted in a later book concerning the times, he called the Rangers the "Mexican-American's Ku Klux Klan. All they need is a white hood with 'Rinches' written across it," he added.

The sentiment was an old one, and his words were most polite and reserved compared to what could be heard privately.

Texas Ranger Ron Stewart (foreground) practices on the Department of Public Safety pistol range in Austin.

Times seem to be quieter, but few earlier years went past without someone, usually a member of the state legislature, calling for the disbanding of the Ranger service. Usually the suggestion was either a summary dismissal of the group or their absorption as "regular" peace officers into the Department of Public Safety.

Frances Farenthold, a reform candidate for governor of Texas campaigning in 1972, called for Ranger dismissal. However confused the rhetoric of civil rights and law enforcement in that decade, the times were not the 1930's. Her stand was considered by some observers to be the most unpopular issue of her unsuccessful campaign.

Still, in occasional years, the Rangers have been accused of personal brutality, taking the law and subsequent justice into their own hands, being strong-arm men against organized labor, using illegal arrest procedures, and committing a host of other evils.

In 1985 and 1986 the Ranger service again was immersed in controversy, this time because of Henry Lee Lucas, an individual who confessed to several hundred murders nationwide. Some law officers working the case were quickly accused of having prompted Lucas with details of the killings — some Lucas apparently could not have done. Texas Attorney General Jim Mattox released a report thereafter claiming that the investigating team had uncritically accepted the confessions, a legal way of saying the job had been bungled, badly. Headlines persisted for months. However, the Public Safety Commission investigated the situation and later reported finding no evidence of wrongdoing on the part of the Ranger service.

But such happenings are rare indeed. When a Ranger was shot to death the next year while apprehending a fugitive suspected of murder and kidnapping, the comments were in praise of the service, even if the news was only news for a couple of days.

The story was typical of the tradition: what better way to apprehend a suspect than to do it face to face—and as soon as possible. Rangers Stan Guffey and John Aycock hid in the back seat of an automobile in which, they thought, the suspect was likely to try a getaway. The Rangers were correct, but the suspect held a two-year-old hostage. The suspect—always the "suspect" in modern-day journalism before a court trial and before a name is released—fired at Ranger Guffey as Aycock grabbed the child. Aycock pushed the child behind him and then "returned the fire" as Guffey slumped, dying. Somewhat later the child was safe, and the suspect and Guffey, the first Ranger killed in the line of duty since 1978, were dead.

Today's Texas Rangers use helicopters more often than horses.

Even border troubles continue. Today parts of Texas' long Rio Grande are beset with situations resembling a grade-B movie. The international line is a profit-making place for those dealing in contraband: drugs going north, weapons going south.

Marijuana, cocaine, heroin, and automatic weapons are the materials of profit—over $20 million worth confiscated in 1987 in the Big Bend area. The quantity involved is now serious enough to engage eight law-enforcing organizations, from federal agents to the county sheriff's department. The Texas Ranger service, naturally, is one of the groups.

Speculation has it that federal agents, notably the Border Patrol, have put so much pressure on Lower Valley crossings that dealers now find the wild country of the Big Bend more attractive.

Events are potent and strange. In the spring of 1987, the time of year when the Chihuahuan desert is in bloom, three Huey helicopters roared south over the Big Bend National Park near Castolon, a former settlement, now a small store, road intersection, and park ranger station. One helicopter landed there, disgorging FBI agents north of the border. The others, carrying Mexican Federal Judicial Police, crossed the river to assault the home of a man called the "czar of narcotics." The target was in the tiny town of Santa Elena, just south of the river. After an hour's gunfight the body of Pablo Acosta was flown away.

The Rangers were not in this fight, but they are close to the situation. Ranger Joaquin Jackson regularly patrols the area and describes the situation with nouns and adjectives usually left out of polite print. He has been quoted as saying that drugs keep the area alive.

Alive, in the last few years, means a private band of mounted, armed men who, when they choose, openly control the San Vicente river crossing in the national park; hundreds of pounds of cocaine confiscated; mutilated bodies in the river; and federal agents who now seem to be in every cafe and on every back road.

Officers in the area have seen enough to confirm a paved runway south of Boquillas, Mexico, which could, and may, handle airplanes loaded with 20,000 pounds of marijuana. Intelligence claims include an antigovernment paramilitary camp south of Lajitas, supported by drug deals, backed by Cuban training. Chinese semiautomatic rifles, converted to automatic fire, have been confiscated, often, on both sides of the border.

It all sounds like a movie. A bad one.

The Rangers on the border are only a tiny fraction of the agents who will deal with the contraband trade. Rangers have always been few compared to other lawmen. Yet, always, they have been in the thick of things. That, probably, will never change.

One reason for their presence is, in fact, that Ranger support is stronger than Ranger criticism. And what criticism there is doesn't bother most Rangers. A retired captain, a veteran of many disputes, once said: "For everyone who don't like me, I got a lot more who do."

The laconic words are apparently true for the whole service.

IMAGES

In Front of the Camera:
Studio and Sky

Photography came to Texas, here and there, between the early 1840's and as late as the next century, depending on where one was standing. Rangers were everywhere, and, like most citizens, were often delighted to pose for the rather interesting, if not downright mysterious, invention.

Itinerant photographers and studio photographers alike had props—some studios were well equipped. Men, in particular, could lead their horses in front of painted backdrops, such as an English cut-stone terrace railing or an Appalachian sunset, then borrow coats, guns, hats, knives—even the horse—to make themselves look a bit more accomplished and prosperous. For this reason, many of these photographs look rather strange today. The gun is often too old for the photograph—the hat doesn't go with the suspenders—one suspects that the coat wasn't much in use outside of Paris. And some early photographic processes produced a mirror image. Men's shirts became buttoned on the wrong side, and the gunslingers had their weaponry close to the hand they used only for cigars.

Clockwise from top right:
Ranger W.W. Collier at age 17 in 1880, "when there were only two kinds of Rangers . . . the quick and the dead"

Charles August Johnson, Company E, Frontier Battalion, 1892

Ranger Capt. John J. Sanders

Possibly A.J. Sowell

117

Clockwise from top right:
Ranger posing with Bowie knife and Colt single-action revolver, from a tintype, c. 1878

Company D at Realitos, 1887: from left, back row—Jim King, "Bass Outlaw," Riley Barton, Charles Fusselman, Mr. Durbin, Ernest Rogers, Charles Barton, Walter Jones; seated—Bob Bell, Capt. Frank Jones, Cal Aten, Walter Durbin, Jim Robinson, and Frank Schmid.

Rangers George Black and ? Britton, Company B, Frontier Battalion

The Panhandle and Central and East Texas

Clockwise from top right:
Texas Rangers at Ranger, Texas

Rangers with Texas National Guard general (center, front), c. 1925

Rangers at Denison, 1922

Plainview, 1890

Clockwise from top right:
*Ranger Headquarters Company,
September 1919:* from left, standing—
*Pvt. Frank Matthews, Jim Martin,
Harrison Hamer, Tom Hickman;
kneeling—Capt. Joe Brooks,
Sgt. Charlie Blackwell, Pvt. Joe Powell,
and Pvt. S.O. Durst.*

*Rangers at Thurber, c. 1890, including
S.M. Graves, Sullivan, Tom Platt,
"Ned" Murphy, Lon Lewis, Thomas,
Malcolm, "Little Mack," S.M. Platt,
and "Red Tom" (Tom O'Hare)*

*Rangers from Company D
at Amarillo, 1891*

*Company D, Frontier Battalion, at
Fort McKavett camp, May 15, 1880*

Ranger at Mexia, 1922

Camps, Cold Camps, and Posts

*R*anger camps, often separate from "headquarters," were always temporary, usually close to wherever Ranger presence was called for, and seldom left much mark.

Headquarters (if Austin was not included) often was a leased private building or house or a donated or commandeered military building with some permanence. With few exceptions, such as Fort Fisher at Waco, Rangers did not establish permanent forts, but they did often camp for extended periods near United States military forts.

When Rangers were on assignment or riding trail, they used whatever shelter came to hand (even a rancher's line cabin might be used) or set up tents (sometimes army surplus, occasionally issue) or used a bedroll like any cowboy on the trail. If the Rangers could set up in an assigned area for any length of time, they used tents for shelters and kitchens and for storage.

For Rangers, a post implied an assignment, not a military garrison; and the cold camp was what it always has been, an overnight without fire—either to accommodate haste or to escape detection.

Considering main settlement areas and common travel routes, Ranger camps might show some kind of pattern, but Rangers set up camp in most parts of Texas. Today nearly every town, city, and crossroads has its tradition of the "Ranger camp" just down the road or the old building once used as a "Ranger jail" or "Ranger headquarters." Some were. By the 1940's, hotels, later motels, were common enough to depend on because much crime had moved to town. Riding the trail had taken on new meaning.

Scenes at Capt. Dan W. Roberts's Ranger camp below Fort McKavett, Menard County, 1878

(Right, center) Capt. Roberts's tent, with Roberts and Sgt. L.P. Sieker standing by the ambulance, 1878

125

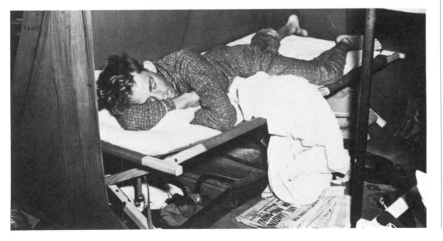

Clockwise from top right:
*Ranger camp at the Kuykendall Ranch,
August 17, 1941*

*Chuck wagon converted from a horse
trailer at a Ranger cattle check camp,
July 30, 1941*

*Sleeping arrangements at the cattle
check camp, July 30, 1941*

*(Center, top) Company B camped on
the San Saba River, September 1896:
from left—Tom Johnson, cook; Allen
Maddox; E.T. Neal; Dudley S. Barker;
and W.J.L. Sullivan.*

*(Center, bottom) Ranger camp near
San Saba*

Company A at Presidio, 1917

*John R. Hughes's Company D, Frontier
Battalion, at Leona, c. 1890*

*Company D, Frontier Battalion, at
Fort McKavett, c. 1880*

*"[At Fort McKavett] the Rangers and
the Yankee soldiers were now neighbors.
The soldiers at Fort McKavett had
never furnished protection against
Indian depredations. Had they afforded
such protection, Company D would not
have been sent there. The soldiers did
not go after the Indians the way the
Rangers did. Their movements were
military, regulated by a lot of red tape,
and they couldn't catch them. The Rangers
used no ceremony; they mounted their
horses, ran down the Indians and killed
them. The soldiers received thirteen
dollars a month; the Rangers received
forty dollars. When a soldier wished to
quit the service before his enlistment
expired, the only way out was to desert;
when a Ranger wanted to quit, his
commander would readily give him a
discharge on the ground that a
dissatisfied Ranger was not efficient.
Rangers had their hearts in the service;
they were protecting the frontier of
their home State. Soldiers and officers
had no social intercourse; Rangers
visited at captain's headquarters, and
were frequently invited to a meal."*

—Mrs. D.W. Roberts

The Trans-Pecos

The Trans-Pecos of present Texas was never in Spanish Texas, nor was it much of a concern to earlier Anglo settlers. It was another world. As part of the immense area east of the Rio Grande claimed by the Republic of Texas, it became a place to settle and use in ways quite different from the motives of either the native Americans or the Spanish.

So far away from the state capital—a journey of weeks over the first Anglo routes into a land of few local lawmen—the area became a region of Ranger activity. Today it is half of the large concern of Company E.

Much of the land is desert, mountain and basin, playa and plain, with abrupt contrasts of plants, animals, and human settlements. The land contains melon fields and silver mines, old volcanoes and dry ocean reefs, lush grasslands and swaths of cactus. The people range from resident Pueblo Indians to northern snowbirds in caravans.

In earlier days the Rangers found the land a beautiful challenge. Here one had to ride trail as efficiently as the Indian. Here reinforcements were too far away to be of consequence. Here many Rangers left their hearts.

Clockwise from top right:
Sgt. Sie Bell and two other Rangers at Langtry, 1918

At Old Deemer's Store on the Rio Grande near Boquillas, 1929:
from left—*Ranger Pete Crawford, Justice of the Peace Ray Miller, Rangers Bob Pool and Arch Miller, and Constable Steve Bennet.*

Capt. C.L. Nevill's camp at Musquiz Creek, Fort Davis, near Alpine, c. 1880 ?

From left—*Ranger Brown's son, Rangers Brown and Wright, Border Patrol Fletcher Rawls, and Rangers H.N. Hall and Buchanan*

San Vicente crossing in the Big Bend region

The Valley

Packing Valley Vegetables for Market.

The Valley of Texas—sometimes called the Lower Valley, the Lower Rio Grande Valley, South Texas, or tropical Texas—is a multicultural river plain stretching up the Rio Grande from the Gulf of Mexico some 150 miles, but certainly south and east of Laredo.

A place called home by more than a dozen native groups, an area of Spanish settlement partly called Nuevo Santander, the Valley culturally encompasses the settlements on both sides of the river, more or less made isolate by strips of brush with infrequent streams to the north and south.

The river was more a crossing and settlement area to the powers of Spain and Mexico, and not a border of Texas, until the Republic of Texas and the United States laid claim to the Nueces Strip.

As a part of Texas, the Valley became a settlement area for Anglos. Here land title was often simply taken as a reward of military conquest, even though both the Republic and State of Texas made provision for the recognition of Spanish land grants. "Native rights" were not even dreamed of.

And a border needed patrolling. State and federal officers did most of the work, but Rangers proved effective as mounted riders to oppose rustlers, smugglers, and thieves (from either side) who would use the border as cover. Rangers seemed less reluctant than some lawmen, certainly more eager than federal troops, to cross an international boundary in hot pursuit.

Today the Valley is a stable society but is still an area where labor disputes, border crossings, and crime can take on the feelings of racial and cultural conflict.

Clockwise from top right:
Capt. J.A. Brooks's Company at the Rio Grande, c. 1891, during the Catarino Garza war

Postcard print of a cockfight by the railway, San Benito, c. 1910's

Capt. J.A. Brooks's Company at Falfurrias, c. 1885

Vegetable harvest in the Valley

131

The Nueces Strip

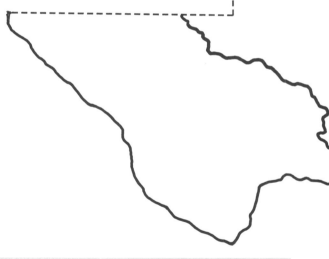

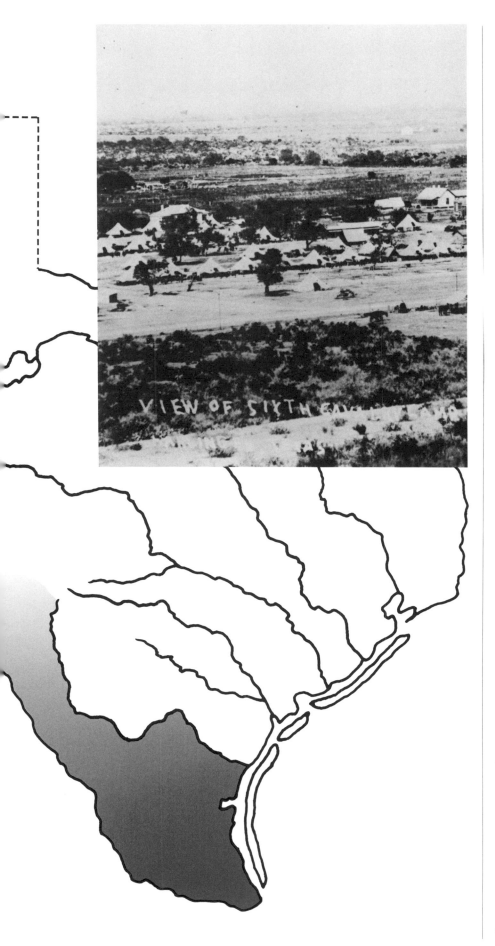

VIEW OF SIXTH CAV

The Nueces Strip, which was mostly an Anglo invention, was more or less the land lying back from the Gulf Coast south of the Nueces River and north of the Rio Grande.

To the Spanish, the Nueces was the southern border of Texas where that province joined Nuevo Santander. The western point of Spanish Texas was where El Moro Creek joined the Nueces in the center of present Dimmit County. Here the Spanish border of Texas turned northeast back to the Medina. For some later arrivals, the "strip" was the narrowest area between the two rivers from Laredo to Del Rio.

Not a part of Spanish Texas, the area was convenient land for the late-coming Anglo-Texians to claim. In particular, with the Rio Grande—the Rio Bravo— as a boundary, half of New Mexico, undefined points north, and such lucrative settlement areas as El Paso and Santa Fe could be considered within Texas. No matter that the Mexican government considered such a claim expansionist madness, the "Mexican War" of the mid-1800's put the question to rest. Texas (and the United States) soon owned the land.

The thinly settled crossroads proved hard to patrol. Bandits of all kinds— and until the 1870's some fragmented Indian groups—found it a haven. And traders snaked their wagons through the brush, no matter what war or border dispute was in progress.

Although a few renegades boasted that the Nueces was a "dead line for sheriffs," the United States military and the Texas Rangers, alongside some of those sheriffs, gradually brought the land into a fairly safe definition of civilization that yielded cattle, sheep, crops, and oil.

Clockwise from top right:
6th Cavalry camp at Harlingen, c. 1915

16th Cavalry on the parade grounds of Fort Brown, Brownsville, c. 1914

Mexican revolutionaries, Piedras Negras and Eagle Pass, 1911

Juan Nepomuceno Cortina, taken when he was governor of Tamaulipas

133

Prohibition and Moonshine

Texas Rangers Moonshiners and Still captured.

Prohibition, the national ban of alcoholic beverage consumption—and most distilling—lasted from 1920 to 1933. Naturally, many people continued to drink and to distill and certainly to bootleg their alcohol right through the period.

The Rangers were given the tasks of aiding federal officers and soldiers in watching the border, destroying illegal stills, and apprehending imbibers. This was duty some Rangers openly disliked, but it was an activity that resulted in many posed photographs.

Making Raid on Moonshiners.

Clockwise from top right:
Rangers and captured moonshiners after a raid in Mexia, c. 1922

Rangers with confiscated contraband, Rio Grande City

Raid on oil-field moonshiners

Smith's Company of Rangers with confiscated bootleg liquor near Tyler, November 9, 1922

Tequila confiscation in Duval County, November 22, 1921

Liquor raid, 1927, with (possibly) William Warren Sterling in the center

Caption on photo:*"The largest destill ever captured in the State of Texas by Rangers. The dimensions are: cooling tank 8' wide by 4' deep—75' of 2" condensing coil—cook off tank 7' by 3'— destilling capacity 32 gal. per hr. or 768 gals. every 24 hrs. @ $8.00 per gal. = $6,144.00—daily income—*

BEATS YOUR OIL WELLS!
Rangers' names and men who assisted in the capture of destill are as follows: left to right—E.L. Young; W.F. Bishop; Rev. Reeves; J.W. Aldrich; A.B. Cummings; Tom Henderson, asst. chief of police; Chas. Purcell, chief, police of Borger; H.B. Purvis; J.W. Bryce; W.P. McConnell; and J.F. McCoy. (Borger, c. 1920.)

Gambling

*G*ambling, as an illegal but public activity in Texas, has always been a Ranger target, often with Rangers operating in tandem with other peace officers.

Many kinds of gambling are hard to hide because they require a place to operate and rather extensive equipment. Thus, gambling, although moderately popular, has always been closely connected with payoffs and local bribes to "the law." Rangers were good "outsiders" who could come into an area to help shut down relatively large operations.

The aftermaths almost always made good photographic studies.

Clockwise from top right:
Rangers with gambling equipment from the Hollywood Club, Galveston, June 20, 1957

Confiscated gambling equipment, July 9, 1953

Rangers burning gambling equipment, December 9, 1948

After a raid in Mexia, c. 1922

139

Gear, Tack, and Rigging

Ranger equipment has varied over the decades, though it usually has been close to that used by regular cowmen and peace officers — but simultaneously.

Rangers have been quick to adopt advances in both armament and gear — when available and affordable — but most of the time have given the impression of operating with the basics: observation and nerve.

Clockwise from top right:
Rangers Dub Taylor, Capt. Olson, and Truman Stone near Round Rock, June 13, 1946

Near Falfurrias, 1932

Alfred Allee and Ab Riggs, 1939

Clockwise from top right:
*Rangers of Company E with equipment,
Midland, November 20, 1970*

On Lake Austin, April 30, 1956

*Ranger exercises with an M4 armored
personnel carrier, c. 1958*

*Rangers with DPS diving equipment,
October 14, 1955*

*Ranger John R. Hughes at the
Department of Public Safety,
examining a Thompson submachine gun,
April 19, 1940*

READINGS

Capt. Jerry Gray's Company B, Big Bend District near Marfa, 1918: from left—Arthur Miles, Capt. Gray, Charles H. Hagler, Bug Barnett, Jack Murdock, Sam Neil, A.G. Beard, Marcus Lanford, Frank Hillbolt, G.W. Cox, Harold King, N.M. Fuller, Frank Crittington, Sgt. A.H. Woelber, and S.F. "Buffalo Bill" Sherman.

This company was formed to replace Capt. Fox's Company, which was disbanded after some of the Rangers entered Mexico with members of the U.S. 8th Cavalry in December 1917 to avenge a border raid. Some of these Rangers had served with Fox.

READINGS

This is not an exhaustive bibliography, nor does it fully represent contemporary research concerning Ranger activity. The Texas Ranger service is becoming a popular subject for academic papers, student presentations, and newspaper features. Likewise, this list is not a compilation of the wealth of Ranger data—files, photographs, records, correspondence, reports—in various collections held by such places as the Department of Public Safety, the Barker Texas History Center, the State Archives, or the material still in private possession.

This is, however, a starting place if one wishes to read of Ranger history, character, and image. Webb is the most revered historian of the service; Gillett and Sterling are often considered to have made the classic statements from the Rangers themselves; Captain and Mrs. Roberts give an interesting set of contrasting remarks about Ranger life; Samora et al. write one of the best presentations of contemporary criticism; Martin and Curry represent the good tradition of modern reporting; Kilgore and Malsch are fine examples of recent biographical works; and the Riglers' book is one of the best.

Nettie Hunter, daughter of J. Marvin Hunter, putting up an advertisement in Bandera for the Texas Rangers' reunion in Menard, 1925

Rangers Buck Weaver, Roy Hardesty, Sgt. Martin N. Koonsman, Warren Belcher, and Tip Eades in East Texas, 1923

Adler, Larry. *The Texas Rangers.* New York: McKay, 1979.

Arrington, A[lfred].W. *The Rangers and Regulators of the Tanaha; or, Life among the Lawless. A Tale of the Republic of Texas.* New York: R.M. DeWitt, 1856; New York: Carleton, 1874.

Aten, Ira. *Six and One-Half Years in the Ranger Service.* Bandera, Tx.: Frontier Times, 1945.

Barry, Buck. *Texas Ranger and Frontiersman.* Ed. James K. Greer. Dallas: Southwest Press, 1932; Lincoln: University of Nebraska Press, 1984.

Barton, Henry W. "The United States Cavalry and the Texas Rangers." *Southwestern Historical Quarterly* 73, no. 4 (April 1960): 495-510.

Castleman, Harvey N. [Vance Randolph.] *The Texas Rangers.* Girard, Kans.: Haldeman-Julius Publications, 1944.

Conger, Roger, et al. *Rangers of Texas.* Waco: Texian Press, 1969.

Cox, Mike. *Silver Stars and Sixguns: The Texas Rangers.* Austin: Texas Department of Public Safety, 1987.

Curry, Jerome P. "Weapons trail leads from Texas to Mexico." *San Antonio Express-News,* April 24, 1988, p. 15-A.

Day, James M. *Captain Clint Peoples, Texas Ranger: Fifty Years a Lawman.* Waco: Texian Press, 1980.

Dobie, James Frank. *A Vaquero of the Brush Country.* Dallas: Southwest Press, 1929 [and many later editions].

Douglas, Claude Leroy. *The Gentlemen in the White Hats: Dramatic Episodes in the History of the Texas Rangers.* Dallas: Southwest Press, 1934.

Durham, George. *On the Trail of 5100 Outlaws.* n.p., 1934.

_____. *Taming the Nueces Strip.* Austin: University of Texas Press, 1962.

Duval, John C[rittenden]. *The Adventures of Big-Foot Wallace, the Texas Ranger and Hunter.* Philadelphia: Claxton, Remsen & Hapfelfinger, 1871; facsimile, Austin: Steck Co., 1947.

_____. *Early Times in Texas.* Austin: H.P.N. Gammel & Co., 1892.

Eckhardt, C.F. "Ballad tells story of trainrobber Bass." *Seguin Gazette-Enterprise,* Wednesday, March 20, 1991, p. 3. [The first in a weekly series of a syndicated column; March 20 and 27, April 3 and 10 deal with the story of Sam Bass.]

Emrich, Duncan. "Cowboy Songs, Ballads, and Cattle Calls from Texas." Sound recording. Washington, D.C.: Library of Congress, Division of Music, 1952.

Ford, John Salmon. *Rip Ford's Texas.* Austin: University of Texas Press, 1963.

Frost, H. Gordon, and John H. Jenkins. *"I'm Frank Hamer"; The Life of a Texas Peace Officer.* Austin: Pemberton Press, 1968.

Gillett, James B. *Six Years with the Texas Rangers, 1875 to 1881*. Foreword by Oliver Knight. Introduction by M.M. Quaife. Lincoln: University of Nebraska Press, 1976. [Earlier edition, Von Boeckmann-Jones Co., Austin, 1921.]

Gilliland, Maude. *Horsebackers of the Brush Country: A Story of the Texas Rangers and Mexican Liquor Smugglers*. Brownsville, Tx.: Springman-King Co., 1968.

Goldstein, Kenneth S. " 'The Texas Rangers' in Aberdeenshire." In *A Good Tale and a Bonny Tune*. Ed. Mody C. Boatright et al. Dallas: SMU Press, 1964.

Greer, James K[immins]. *Colonel Jack Hays: Texas Frontier Leader and California Builder*. New York: Dutton, 1952; rev. ed., College Station: Texas A&M University Press, 1987.

Grinstead, J.F. *Texas Ranger Justice*. New York: Dodge, 1941.

Henderson, Harry McCorry. *Colonel Jack Hays, Texas Ranger*. San Antonio: Naylor Co., 1954.

Henry, Will. *The Texas Rangers*. New York: Random House, 1957.

House, Edward Mandell. *Riding for Texas*. New York: John Day, 1936.

Hughes, William J. *Rebellious Ranger: Rip Ford and the Old Southwest*. Norman: University of Oklahoma Press, 1964.

Hunter, J[ohn]. Marvin, ed. *Jack Hays: The Intrepid Texas Ranger*. Bandera, Tx.: Frontier Times, [1920?].

Ingmire, Frances Terry. *Texas Ranger Service Records, 1847-1900*. St. Louis: Ingmire, 1982.

Jennings, Napoleon Augustus. *A Texas Ranger*. New York: Scribner's Sons, 1899; facsimile, Austin: Steck Co., 1959.

Jensen, Ann, ed. *Texas Ranger's Diary*. Dallas: Kaleidograph, 1936.

Jones, John B. *Report of Maj. J.B. Jones, Commanding the Frontier Battalion, Texas State Troops, March, 1876*. Houston: A.C. Gray, state printer, 1876.

Kilgore, Daniel Edmond. *A Ranger Legacy: 150 Years of Service to Texas*. Austin: Madrona Press, 1973.

Malsch, Brownson. *Captain M.T. Lone Wolf Gonzaullas, The Only Texas Ranger Captain of Spanish Descent*. Austin: Shoal Creek Publishers, 1980.

Maltby, William J. *Captain Jeff, or, Frontier Life in Texas with the Texas Rangers*. Colorado, Tx.: Whipkey Printing Co., 1906; Waco: Texian Press, 1967.

Martin, Gary. "Millions in drugs cross at Big Bend." *San Antonio Express News*, April 24, 1988, pp. 1-A, 14-A.

Martin, Jack. *Border Boss, Captain John R. Hughes, Texas Ranger*. San Antonio: Naylor Co., 1942.

Company A, Harlingen, 1904, from left – two unidentified Rangers, Bill McCawley, Capt. Frank Johnson, Crosley Marsden, Oscar Roundtree, and Gus T. "Buster" Jones.

Capt. Bill McMurray

Company D at Alice, December 1943: standing, from left—Alfred Allee, Zeno Smith, Leon Vivian, Joe Bridge, Robert Rohatsch; seated— Capt. Gully Cowert, Frank Mills, and John Hensley.

Mason-Manheim, Madeline. *Riding for Texas: The True Adventures of Captain Bill McDonald of the Texas Rangers.* New York: Reynal & Hitchcock, 1936.

Mayo, Earl. *The Texas Rangers: The Most Efficient Police Force in the World.* New York: F. Leslie Publishing House, 1901. [From *Frank Leslie's Popular Monthly,* October 1901.]

Oates, Stephen B. *Visions of Glory, Texans on the Southwestern Frontier.* Norman: University of Oklahoma Press, [1970].

Ogden, George Washington. *The Watch on the Rio Grande.* New York, 1911. [From *Everybody's Magazine,* September 1911.]

Paine, Albert Bigelow. *Captain Bill McDonald, Texas Ranger.* New York: J.J. Little & Ives, 1909; Austin: State House Press, 1985.

Paredes, Américo. *"With His Pistol in His Hand."* Austin: University of Texas Press, 1958.

Pike, James. *Scout and Ranger.* 1865; Cincinnati: Hawley, 1965; New York: Da Capo Press, 1972.

Preece, Harold. *Lone Star Man: Ira Aten, Last of the Old Texas Rangers.* New York: Hastings House, 1960.

Proctor, Ben H. "The Modern Texas Rangers: A Law-Enforcement Dilemma in the Rio Grande Valley." In *The Mexican Americans: An Awakening Minority.* Ed. Manuel P. Servin. Beverly Hills: Glencoe Press, 1970.

Raymond, Dora Neill. *Captain Lee Hall of Texas.* Norman: University of Oklahoma Press, 1940.

Reid, Samuel Chester. *The Scouting Expeditions of McCulloch's Texas Rangers.* Philadelphia, 1847, 1859; Austin: Steck Co., 1935.

Rigler, Lewis C., and Judyth Wagner Rigler. *In the Line of Duty: Reflections of a Texas Ranger Private.* Houston: Larksdale Press, 1984.

Roberts, Dan W., and Lou Conway [Mrs. D.W.] Roberts. *Rangers and Sovereignty by Dan W. Roberts. A Woman's Reminiscences of Six Years in Camp with the Texas Rangers by Mrs. D.W. Roberts.* Intro. Robert Wooster. Austin: State House Press, 1987. [Facsimile ed. of the originals, combined in one volume. First work originally published San Antonio: Wood Printing & Engraving Co., 1914; second work originally published Austin: Von Boeckmann-Jones Co., (1928?).]

Samora, Julian; Joe Bernal, and Albert Peña. *Gunpowder Justice: A Reassessment of the Texas Rangers.* Notre Dame: University of Notre Dame Press, 1979.

Servin, Manuel P., ed. *The Mexican-Americans: An Awakening Minority.* Beverly Hills: Glencoe Press, 1970. [See, among others, the article by B.H. Proctor noted above.]

Sinise, Jerry. *George Washington Arrington: Civil War Spy, Texas Ranger, Sheriff, and Rancher; a Biography.* Burnet, Tx.: Eakin Press, 1979.

Smithwick, Noah. *The Texas Rangers, 1836-1839.* Houston: Union National Bank, 1933; Austin: Steck Co., 1935; Austin: University of Texas Press, 1983. [Extract from *The Evolution of a State.*]

Sowell, A[ndrew].J[ackson]. *Early Settlers and Indian Fighters.* Austin: State House Books, 1986.

_____. *Life of "Big Foot" Wallace.* 189?; facsimile, Austin: Steck Co., 1957; Austin: State House Press, 1989.

_____. *Rangers and Pioneers of Texas.* New York: Argosy-Antiquarian, 1964. [Reprinted from the 1884 edition.]

Stephens, Robert W. *Lone Wolf: The Story of Texas Ranger Captain M.T. Gonzaullas.* Dallas: Taylor Publishing Co., [1979?].

_____. *Texas Ranger Sketches.* Dallas: privately printed, 1972.

_____. *Tribute to a Ranger: Captain Alfred Y. Allee.* n.p, 1968.

Sterling, William Warren. *Trails and Trials of a Texas Ranger.* Norman: University of Oklahoma Press, 1968. [Earlier edition, n.p., 1959.]

Sullivan, W.J[ohn].L. *Twelve Years in the Saddle for Law and Order on the Frontiers of Texas.* New York: Buffalo-Head Press, 1966 [copyright 1909].

Texas Department of Public Safety. *Texas Rangers.* Austin, 1954. [An account of the history of the founding and activities of the Texas Rangers with an appended chronological index.]

Walker, Samuel Hamilton. *Samuel H. Walker's Account of the Mier Expedition.* Ed., intro. Marilyn McAdams Sibley. Austin: Texas State Historical Association, 1978.

Webb, Walter Prescott. *The Story of the Texas Rangers.* New York: Grosset & Dunlap, 1957; Austin: Encino Press, 1971. Juvenile.

_____. *The Texas Rangers: A Century of Frontier Defense.* Boston: Houghton Mifflin, 1935; Austin: University of Texas Press, 1965; reprint, 1980.

Capt. Buck Barry (1821-1906)

Saloon in Louise, Texas, early 1900's

PHOTO CREDITS

A Texas Ranger poses for a publicity photograph. c. 1928.

PHOTO CREDITS

Nearly all of the photographs are from the collections of The University of Texas Institute of Texan Cultures at San Antonio (ITC), courtesy of the following lenders. Credits of photos from left to right are divided by semicolons and from top to bottom by dashes.

Ranger William G. King with unidentified woman and dog

Austin; Arnulfo L. Oliveira Memorial Library, Texas Southmost College, Brownsville –

line 3: All four from Texas Department of Public Safety Collection, Texas State Library, Austin –

line 4: Western History Collections, University of Oklahoma at Norman; next three from Texas Department of Public Safety Collection, Texas State Library, Austin.

6   Western History Collections, University of Oklahoma at Norman.

7   Harry Ransom Humanities Research Center, University of Texas at Austin.

8   Eugene C. Barker Texas History Center, University of Texas at Austin.

11   Francis P. Moore Jr., *Map and Description of Texas: Containing Sketches of Its History, Geology, Geography and Statistics* (Philadelphia: H. Tanner Junr.; New York: Tanner & Disturnell, 1840).

12   Zintgraff Collection, ITC; Noah Smithwick, *The Evolution of a State* (Austin: H.P.N. Gammel, 1900).

13   José Cisneros, El Paso.

14   ITC.

15   R.Q. Sutherland, *The Book of Colt Firearms* (Kansas City, Mo.: n.d.).

16   Texas State Capitol, Austin.

17   J.W. Wilbarger, *Indian Depredations in Texas* (Austin: Hutchings Printing House, 1889).

18   Frontier Times Museum, Bandera.

19   Library of Congress, Washington.

20   Ellen Schulz Quillin Collection, ITC – (inset) Texian Press, Waco – Henry Barnard, *Armsmear: the Home, the Arm and the Armory of Samuel Colt* (New York, 1866).

23   Gonzales Memorial Museum, Gonzales.

24   Amanda Ochse, San Antonio.

25   Library of the Daughters of the Republic of Texas at the Alamo – ITC; *San Antonio Daily Express*, May 26, 1894 – *Frank Leslie's Illustrated Newspaper* (New York, 1859).

26   Bruce Marshall, Austin.

28   Terrell Maverick Webb, San Antonio; Bruce Marshall, Austin.

29   ITC (replica loaned by IMAX Theater) – Bruce Marshall, Austin.

30   Texian Press, Waco.

31   Texian Press, Waco.

32   Western History Collections, University of Oklahoma at Norman; ITC.

33   Catherine McDowell, San Antonio.

34   Charles T. Haven and Frank A. Belden, *A History of the Colt Revolver* (New York: William Morrow & Co., 1940).

36   L.J. Wortham, *A History of Texas* (Fort Worth: Wortham-Molyneaux Co., 1924).

37   Texas State Capitol, Austin.

38   Western History Collections, University of Oklahoma at Norman.

39   Arnulfo L. Oliveira Memorial Library, Texas Southmost College, Brownsville.

40   William H. Emory, *Report on the U.S. & Mexican Boundary Survey . . . Secretary of the Interior* (Washington, D.C., 1857).

41   Bruce Marshall, Austin.

42   Roger Conger, Waco.

44   Archives Division, Texas State Library, Austin.

47   Eugene C. Barker Texas History Center, University of Texas at Austin.

48   Western History Collections, University of Oklahoma at Norman.

50   Western History Collections, University of Oklahoma at Norman; Texas Department of Public Safety Collection, Texas State Library, Austin.

51   Lewis E. Daniell, *Personnel of the Texas State Government* (San Antonio: Maverick Printing Company, 1892).

52   Western History Collections, University of Oklahoma at Norman.

53   Arnulfo L. Oliveira Memorial Library, Texas Southmost College,

Rangers at Brownsville, c. 1910, as identified by R.C. Schmelling: standing, from left – detective from Indiana, James B. Wells, detective, unknown Ranger, Henry Lawrence, Frank Baker; seated – Capt. Fox, Henry Agar, and Capt. Wright (?).

Brownsville—Western History Collections, University of Oklahoma at Norman.

54 Both from Western History Collections, University of Oklahoma at Norman.

55 Western History Collections, University of Oklahoma at Norman.

56 Western History Collections, University of Oklahoma at Norman.

57 Western History Collections, University of Oklahoma at Norman.

58 Western History Collections, University of Oklahoma at Norman.

60 Texas Department of Public Safety Collection, Texas State Library, Austin.

61 Terrell Maverick Webb, San Antonio.

62 William H. Emory, *Report on the U.S. & Mexican Boundary Survey . . . Secretary of the Interior* (Washington, D.C., 1857).

63 San Antonio Conservation Society, San Antonio.

64 Texas Department of Public Safety Collection, Texas State Library, Austin.

66 Western History Collections, University of Oklahoma at Norman.

67 Western History Collections, University of Oklahoma at Norman.

68 Western History Collections, University of Oklahoma at Norman.

69 Texian Press, Waco.

70 Western History Collections, University of Oklahoma at Norman.

71 Western History Collections, University of Oklahoma at Norman.

72 Texas Department of Public Safety Collection, Texas State Library, Austin.

73 Both from Western History Collections, University of Oklahoma at Norman.

74 Western History Collections, University of Oklahoma at Norman.

76 Both from Western History Collections, University of Oklahoma at Norman.

77 Both from Western History Collections, University of Oklahoma at Norman.

78 Western History Collections, University of Oklahoma at Norman.

80 Western History Collections, University of Oklahoma at Norman.

81 Used with the permission of William J. Helmer, *The Gun that Made the Twenties Roar* (New York: Macmillan Publishing Co., 1969).

82 Van der Stucken Family, San Antonio.

84 Fort Sam Houston Military Museum, San Antonio.

85 Arnulfo L. Oliveira Memorial Library, Texas Southmost College, Brownsville.

86 Western History Collections, University of Oklahoma at Norman; Texas Department of Public Safety Collection, Texas State Library, Austin.

87 Clara Zepeda, San Benito.

88 Arnulfo L. Oliveira Memorial Library, Texas Southmost College, Brownsville.

89 Arnulfo L. Oliveira Memorial Library, Texas Southmost College, Brownsville.

90 Texas Department of Public Safety Collection, Texas State Library, Austin.

91 Texas Department of Public Safety Collection, Texas State Library, Austin.

92 Western History Collections, University of Oklahoma at Norman.

93 Texas Department of Public Safety Collection, Texas State Library, Austin.

94 *Texas Rangers* Magazine (New York: Better Publishing Co., May 1954).

96 Texas Department of Public Safety Collection, Texas State Library, Austin.

97 Bank of the Southwest, Frank J. Schlueter Collection, Houston Metropolitan Research Center, Houston Public Library.

98 Harry Ransom Humanities Research Center, University of Texas at Austin.

100 Western History Collections, University of Oklahoma at Norman.

John Cotulla and Ranger Jim Wright in Cotulla

Ranger Dub Taylor with full gear, including dogs, horse, and trailer, September 27, 1939

Rangers Honeycutt and Trimble, 1923

A Ranger exchanges a message with a helicopter pilot during training and exercises at Camp Hood, October 18, 1949. The maneuver may have been carried out only in practice.

102 Texas Department of Public Safety Collection, Texas State Library, Austin.

103 Western History Collections, University of Oklahoma at Norman – Texas Department of Public Safety Collection, Texas State Library, Austin.

104 Texas Department of Public Safety Collection, Texas State Library, Austin.

106 Archives Division, Texas State Library, Austin.

107 Texas Department of Public Safety Collection, Texas State Library, Austin.

108 Texas Department of Public Safety Collection, Texas State Library, Austin.

109 Archives Division, Texas State Library, Austin.

110 Texas Department of Public Safety Collection, Texas State Library, Austin.

111 Texas Department of Public Safety Collection, Texas State Library, Austin.

113 Texas Department of Public Safety Collection, Texas State Library, Austin.

115 Texas Department of Public Safety Collection, Texas State Library, Austin.

116 Western History Collections, University of Oklahoma at Norman.

117 Western History Collections, University of Oklahoma at Norman – next two from Archives Division, Texas State Library, Austin.

118 Texas Department of Public Safety Collection, Texas State Library, Austin.

119 William D. Wittliff, Austin – Western History Collections, University of Oklahoma at Norman.

120 Both from Texas Department of Public Safety Collection, Texas State Library, Austin.

121 ITC – Texas Department of Public Safety Collection, Texas State Library, Austin.

122 Texas Department of Public Safety Collection, Texas State Library, Austin.

123 Western History Collections, University of Oklahoma at Norman – next three from Texas Department of Public Safety Collection, Texas State Library, Austin.

124 Both from Western History Collections, University of Oklahoma at Norman.

125 All three from Western History Collections, University of Oklahoma at Norman.

126 Top three from Western History Collections, University of Oklahoma at Norman – Hugh C. Cole Jr., Donna, Texas; *San Antonio Express-News*.

127 All three from Texas Department of Public Safety Collection, Texas State Library, Austin.

128 ITC – Heritage Museum, Falfurrias.

129 Texas Department of Public Safety Collection, Texas State Library, Austin – next two from W.D. Smithers Collection, Harry Ransom Humanities Research Center, University of Texas at Austin.

130 Harlingen Public Library, Harlingen.

131 Texas Department of Public Safety Collection, Texas State Library, Austin – Estate of Ford Green, San Antonio – Western History Collections, University of Oklahoma at Norman.

132 First two from Fort Sam Houston Military Museum, San Antonio; José T. Canales, *Juan N. Cortina: Bandit or Patriot?* (San Antonio: Artes Graficas, 1851) – next two from Fort Sam Houston Military Museum, San Antonio; Arnulfo L. Oliveira Memorial Library, Texas Southmost College, Brownsville.

133 Harlingen Public Library, Harlingen.

134 Western History Collections, University of Oklahoma at Norman – next two from Texas Department of Public Safety Collection, Texas State Library, Austin.

135 Western History Collections, University of Oklahoma at Norman – Hugh C. Cole Jr., Donna, Texas – Western History Collections, University of Oklahoma at Norman.
136 Texas Department of Public Safety Collection, Texas State Library, Austin.
138 Western History Collections, University of Oklahoma at Norman.
139 All three from Texas Department of Public Safety Collection, Texas State Library, Austin.
140 Texas Department of Public Safety Collection, Texas State Library, Austin – Western History Collections, University of Oklahoma at Norman.
141 Texas Department of Public Safety Collection, Texas State Library, Austin.
142 Both from Texas Department of Public Safety Collection, Texas State Library, Austin.
143 All three from Texas Department of Public Safety Collection, Texas State Library, Austin.
145 Western History Collections, University of Oklahoma at Norman.
146 W.D. Smithers Collection, Harry Ransom Humanities Research Center, University of Texas at Austin.
148 W.D. Smithers Collection, Harry Ransom Humanities Research Center, University of Texas at Austin – Western History Collections, University of Oklahoma at Norman.
149 Western History Collections, University of Oklahoma at Norman.
150 Both from Heritage Museum, Falfurrias.
151 S.W. Pease, San Antonio – Wharton County Historical Museum, Wharton.
153 Texas Department of Public Safety Collection, Texas State Library, Austin.
154 Texas Department of Public Safety Collection, Texas State Library, Austin.
156 Victor Friedricks, Austin – Arnulfo L. Oliveira Memorial Library, Texas Southmost College, Brownsville.
157 John Cotulla, Cotulla, Texas – Texas Department of Public Safety Collection, Texas State Library, Austin.
158 Hugh C. Cole Jr., Donna, Texas – Texas Department of Public Safety Collection, Texas State Library, Austin.
159 Both from Archives Division, Texas State Library, Austin.
161 Texas Department of Public Safety Collection, Texas State Library, Austin.
162 Lillie S. Schuchardt, Kendall County.
164 *San Antonio Light* Collection, ITC – Mrs. Charles C. Bush III, San Antonio.
165 Texas Department of Public Safety Collection, Texas State Library, Austin – Archives Division, Texas State Library, Austin.
166 Archives Division, Texas State Library, Austin – Texas Department of Public Safety Collection, Texas State Library, Austin.
167 Heritage Museum, Falfurrias.
168 Both from Texas Department of Public Safety Collection, Texas State Library, Austin.
169 Western History Collections, University of Oklahoma at Norman.
170 Western History Collections, University of Oklahoma at Norman – Archives Division, Texas State Library, Austin.
171 Texas Department of Public Safety Collection, Texas State Library, Austin.
Map
 Left Wharton County Historical Museum, Wharton – Texas Parks and Wildlife Department, Austin.
Right Texas Department of Public Safety Collection, Texas State Library, Austin – John Wildenthal Family, Cotulla, Texas – Texas Department of Public Safety Collection, Texas State Library, Austin – ITC.

Rangers at Glenn Spring, 1919

Rangers of Company E, Frontier Battalion: from left – Sergeant Guede Britton; Johnnie Snyder, cook; Jeff Mankins; Rob Pease; John L. Sullivan; Mat "Darling" A. Buns; and Welsey W. Cates.

INDEX

Henry M. Smith, San Antonio marshal and former Texas Ranger, with his wife, Frances Short, c. 1868. The woman in the center is unidentified.

INDEX

Italic page numbers indicate photographs.

The Jersey Lilly Saloon in Langtry, with Judge Roy Bean holding court, trying a horse thief. c. 1890

The Jersey Lilly Saloon abandoned, c. 1910's

Tom Hickman, July 1942

Rangers at Glenn Spring, 1919

Lt. Jim Gillespie, Company E

Rangers L.H. Purvis and Clint Peoples checking cattle at Kerrville, June 24, 1949

Homer White, age 23—Ranger in Capt. Johnson's Company, 1908

Rangers of Company D in a gas mask drill, Fort Sam Houston, March 31 1971

Dr. Paul B. Hill, Chaplin of the Texas Rangers, San Antonio, October 18, 1938

Capt. Sam McMurry, c. 1889

Nat B. "Kiowa" Jones, Menard, 1927

Rangers at a wedding (?), Glenn Spring, 1919

Everywhere in Texas . . .

If every Texas Ranger battle, post, grave, assignment, headquarters, chase, investigation, and scout were put on a single map, nearly every Texas city, town, river, mountain range, fort, county, hill, and creek would be represented. Some small settlements claim notice beyond their present-day prominence: there are, for example, those who say Center Point (the one in Kerr County) might have the largest number of Ranger burials per graveyard. Scabb (either one) is not really there anymore; San Felipe de Austin really wasn't ever Ranger headquarters, and Waco's former red light district is now politely considered fiction.

This map, therefore, is for orientation and initial curiosity. It lists only the main sites mentioned in this book—a sampling of Ranger activity. The best way to know the locations is to walk the land; and that, in some places, can still be done.

Texas Rangers Company Areas

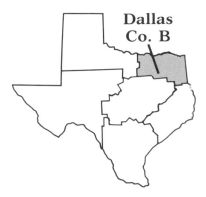

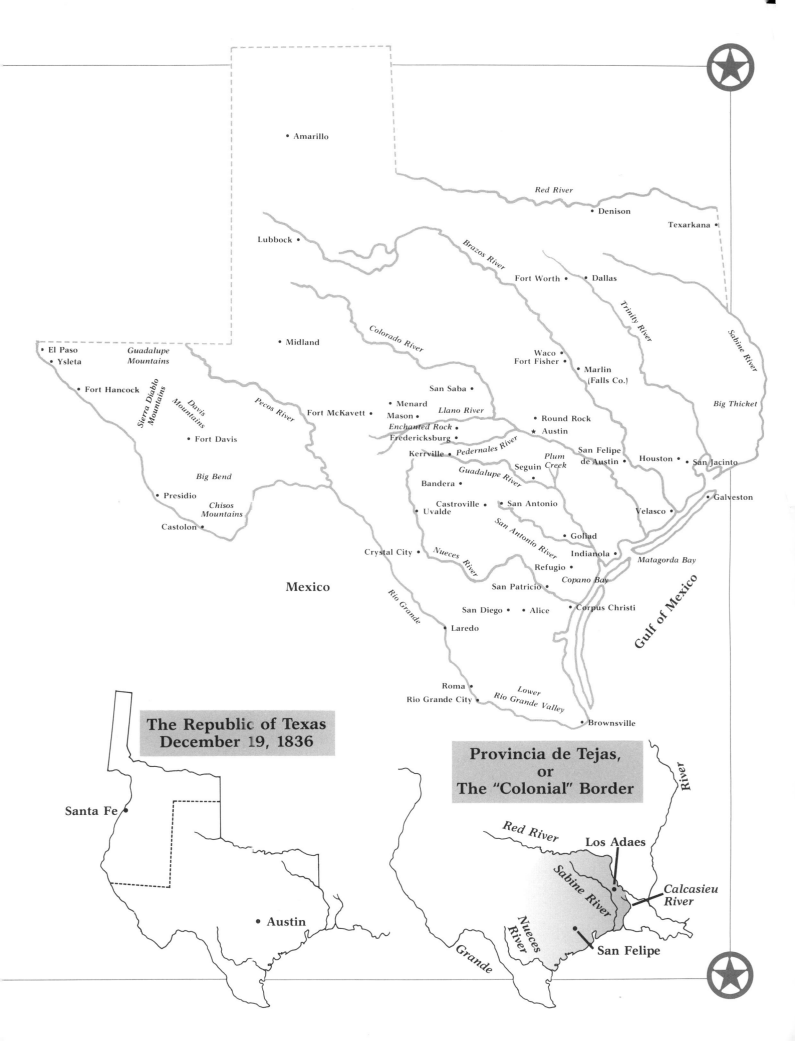

Amarillo

Red River

Denison

Texarkana

Lubbock

Brazos River

Fort Worth • Dallas

Trinity River

Sabine River

El Paso
Ysleta

Guadalupe
Mountains

Midland

Colorado River

Waco
Fort Fisher

Marlin
(Falls Co.)

Big Thicket

Fort Hancock

Sierra Diablo Mountains

Davis
Mountains

Pecos River

Fort McKavett

San Saba

Menard
Mason

Llano River

Enchanted Rock
Fredericksburg

Round Rock

Austin

San Felipe
de Austin

Houston • San Jacinto

Fort Davis

Big Bend

Kerrville

Pedernales River

Seguin

Plum
Creek

Castroville
Uvalde

Guadalupe River

Bandera

San Antonio

Velasco

Galveston

Presidio

Chisos
Mountains

Castolon

Crystal City

Nueces River

San Antonio River

Goliad

Indianola

Matagorda Bay

Refugio

Copano Bay

Gulf of Mexico

Mexico

Rio Grande

San Patricio

San Diego • Alice

Corpus Christi

Laredo

Roma

Rio Grande City

Lower
Rio Grande Valley

Brownsville

The Republic of Texas
December 19, 1836

Santa Fe

Austin

Provincia de Tejas,
or
The "Colonial" Border

River

Red River

Los Adaes

Sabine River

Calcasieu
River

Nueces
River

San Felipe

Grande

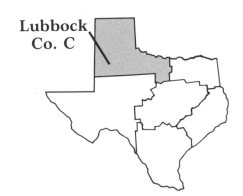

Lubbock
Co. C

San Antonio
Co. D

Midland
Co. E

Waco
Co. F

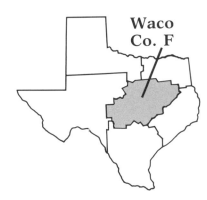